The Village's Boy

JESUS C. TORRES

WESTBOW
P R E S S®
A DIVISION OF THOMAS NELSON
& ZONDERVAN

WestBow Press books may be ordered through booksellers or by contacting:

WestBow Press
A Division of Thomas Nelson & Zondervan
1663 Liberty Drive
Bloomington, IN 47403
www.westbowpress.com
1 (866) 928-1240

ISBN: 978-1-9736-5252-6 (sc)
ISBN: 978-1-9736-5254-0 (hc)
ISBN: 978-1-9736-5253-3 (e)

Library of Congress Control Number: 2019901094

Print information available on the last page.

WestBow Press rev. date: 02/13/2019

MY DEEPEST GRATITUDE TO ...

My heavenly Father, His Son Jesus Christ, and the Holy Spirit.

To the memory of my father and my mother.

To my wife, Ingrid, for the gift she has given me: two daughters and a son. Regardless the situation, she has been there doing the things that a wife is supposed to do.

Sharon, my firstborn, has come a long way in doing the things she wants to do. She graduated from college and is on her way to practicing law.

Tracy, my second daughter, who also finished college and is happily working in her field.

Jesse, my son, just finished high school and is getting ready to begin his career. He was one of the people who encouraged me to write this book. He had the opportunity to open the curtain for a swift moment on my past and awoke what it had been in me for a long time—along with others who had also encouraged me to tell my story.

CONTENTS

PREFACE

This book is my story and the story of those who cannot tell their own stories because their lives were snatched away. What you are about to read will have a great impact on your life—just as it has had on mine. It is based on a real story. I have served God almost all my life and have experienced His love firsthand. I have no other desire than to magnify my heavenly Father's name through His Son Jesus.

My only desire is that when this book gets into your hands, you will start to see your Christian life in the way God has intended for you to live it. Perhaps you will see that so much of what you have heard about God, has never made that impact that is needed in someone's life. Now you will be able to be a witness of the power of God. Then, like Job, you will be able to say, "I heard of you by the hearing of the ear, but now my eye sees you."

It is time to begin the relationship your soul has always longed for. Since you were created to be an ambassador of the kingdom of heaven, how many times have you fallen short of representing your King? How many times have you felt the need—but haven't done anything because you did not know how. There are other times when you had an opportunity to tell others who you are, but you failed to do so because you lacked the part that propels you to convey the message you are supposed to deliver. At other times, you don't give things the importance that is required from above.

Putting these factors together, we will see that there is a gap that needs to be filled. It is the essential part that all Christians need to incorporate into their lives. That part brings us closer to God. I have gone to many parts of the world, and the one thing I have seen in common among Christians is that they are accustomed to following traditions and not being in touch with the real meaning of the call that everyone is commanded to follow.

It is so simple to ignore the commandment given by Jesus:

> Go ye therefore, and teach all nations, baptizing them in the name of the Father, and of the Son, and of the Holy Ghost. (Mathew 28:19)

I was doing a job for some people when the phone rang. The person looked at the call display and decided not to answer. The answering machine picked up the call, and it was a church letting the person know a woman was in need of prayer. The person was asked to pray for her.

When I heard that, I was compelled to say, "Do you believe in God?"

"Yes," she replied.

I said, "Why you believe in God?"

She said "Because God had answered all my prayers."

I had spent two days in that house, and if not for that phone call, I wouldn't have known that person was a follower of Christ.

We see the same picture throughout the Christian community. In most cases, we have treated the scriptures like mythological stories and do not value the power that resides within them. That's why so many people are oppressed by the enemy. That's why they are going to churches and expecting to be accepted just the way they are without being born again. We are missing that message of Elijah, and that message of John the Baptist.

I heard a pastor saying that John the Baptist lost his head on his own account—in other words, he was preaching a message God hadn't sent him to preach. The scripture says:

> Therefore to him that knoweth to do good, and doeth it not, to him it is sin. (James 4:17)

> Therefore, we are commended to speak the truth so in that day when the Great Judge calls us to face Him, we hear Him say, "Come, ye blessed of my Father, inherit

the kingdom prepared for you from the foundation of the world." (Matthew 25:34)

I was spared by that brutal civil war that lasted for more than twelve years in El Salvador because God had a plan for my life. There were times when my faith seemed to fade away. I thought, *why am I on the run if I haven't done anything wrong?*

I learned to trust God. Whatever happened, I knew He was always walking alongside me. When I didn't understand what was going on—or when I didn't fully comprehend His will for my life—I never stop believing that things were going to get better. Everything I am, I owe to the Lord because He took me in when I was left fatherless at an early age. I don't pretend to have reached it all, but the more I seek Him, the more I find out how much He loves me. I have learned not to worry about the things I don't understand because they belong to Him.

INTRODUCTION

And we know that all things work together
for good to them that love God, to them who
are the called according to his purpose.
—Romans 8:28

Have you lived in a place where you think there is no other place like it? Perhaps it is where we get the expression "there is no place like home," and that is exactly what happened to me when I was growing up. I thought my place of birth was all I needed—and that I had no need to ever leave and settle in another place.

The Village's Boy is packed with those good and bad stories from my childhood. I experienced good times and bad times growing up with my siblings. There are nine of us, and a large community that all knew each other. We believed that living in harmony kept us going even when there were others with different beliefs. The Christian community was about 25 percent and increasing. We had plans to build a church since there was no church building before the destruction began.

The Village's Boy illustrates the atrocities committed against innocent people, including the author. The names of the characters in the story are fictional to protect the names of the real characters who are no longer living. The only fault that caused their death was that they believed their government was there to protect them, and it turned out that they were the aggressors. They felt protected by the very ones who took their lives without remorse.

People have asked so many questions. Some questioned why God let these things happen. Others asked, "Where was God when those killers were killing innocent people? Why didn't He do anything? That way, we could believe there is a God!" It is a natural way for people to think humanly, but the truth of the matter is that—even when we don't understand why things happen the way they happen—we have to trust God. We will feel a sense of justice, and even when we can't see the future, we know God will provide a way out of the situation. God will transform evil for good, and everything will work out for the best.

God loves His children. Even when you think God has abandoned you and you don't hear His voice, don't worry. He hasn't gone away. He's still in control—and you are not alone. You will see that His promises are true. He really meant it when He said, "I will not leave you comfortless: I will come to you" (John 14:18).

CHAPTER 1

My Childhood

My childhood is full of good memories. Since I'm the eighth child in my family, there was a lot going on all the time. I have six sisters and two brothers. When I was growing up, the two oldest ones were established with families of their own. The rest of us lived at home. I don't remember much about my oldest sister because she moved to another village and had two kids of her own. I didn't connect with her as I did with the others.

Nonetheless, it was cool to go on the occasional journey to see my big sister. She enjoyed having me visit her because she would have someone for her two kids to play with. Every time I went to her place, we had to make plans and discuss who was going. Some of us had chores to do, and my mother had to decide who deserved to get out of the house since it was like a vacation.

There was always work to do. If I wasn't working in

the fields with my father, I was taking care of livestock. If there was a chance to leave home—even for only a day—it was worth it. We had to walk for at least two hours to get to my sister's, but we enjoyed it because we could do fun stuff along the way. When I went with the sister who is only a year older than me, we stopped at the house of a lady who had a parrot. That parrot was so funny. We could spend hours listening to her singing. She used to climb into some orange trees that were facing the road to interact with people. She was like a person. She had been trained very well. We could talk to her, and she would make us laugh. One time, one of my friends fell flat on the ground while laughing because the bird was mimicking everything he did.

When I was about seven years old, school only lasted half the day. I got to play a little more than the rest of my siblings. Even when I didn't have any toys, I found ways to entertain myself. When it came to connecting with my nephews, it was awesome. We used to make our own toys by using whatever we could find lying around. There is a plant called *Tarro,* and it grows like the watermelon vine—but it reaches at least fifty pounds. We used them for everything from carrying water to storing all the grain for cooking. When they were ripe, they were split in half with a handsaw. Ashes were poured in so the inside would rot. Within a week, the bowl was cleaned out and ready to use. This was the material we used to make the wheels for the little toy cars, and using sticks as axels. Since I didn't have any tools to make my toys, I used my mom's kitchen knife.

I played with my nephews, and there were lots of fruits we could eat. Regardless of the season, there was always something to get in the woods. We enjoyed a patch of cashew trees that was almost abandoned. Sometimes the only company we had were birds. We ate the fruit and saved the nuts for later. Part of the fun was climbing the trees and challenging each other to see who could climb higher. We had a competition to see who could get the best cashew fruit. It is more fun eating a cashew fruit than eating the roasted nut. That was the first part of the fun. After we showed off how much we had collected, it was time to roast them. We gathered rocks and put them in the shape of a U. to build a structure, so we could make a fire. Then it was time to figure out where to find a piece of metal or a piece of clay pot to do the roasting of the nuts.

We sometimes had access to sugarcane. Sugarcane, mangos, and many other fruits were very popular throughout that region, but the cashew trees are amazing. The trees produce fruits during the dry season. Many parts of the Americas only have two seasons. Summer lasts six long months—without rain—and winter is the rainy season. The cashew trees wait until all the vegetation is completely withered before they blossom. The rain interferes with the development of the fruit. When there was an early rainfall, the fruit would get a plague. For the kids, this was amazing because we always had something to eat.

We were excited for the sugarcane to be processed. The sugarcane was prepped for processing from the beginning of December until the end of February. It was a great deal for us because of the free sugary drinks and all the derivatives of the cane. It was an important industry for the region.

The villages were self-sufficient. Almost every villager owned a piece of land, and villagers had very little dependency on the outside world. The houses were separated by great distances, and there was enough space to grow crops.

People produced everything they needed to survive—from coffee to the sugar needed to sweeten it. The few things they didn't have were salt and clothes, but some people even fabricated their own shoes. Our only close neighbors were my grandparents. They lived about a block away, and my father's youngest sister, her husband, and their five kids lived with them. Two uncles lived at their house, and one of them was married and had four kids. Everywhere I turned, I had people surrounding me.

The time came when I had to say goodbye to my oldest sister, three nephews, and a baby niece. They were moving to a different part of the country in search of a better life. That was completely out of the question for the rest of us because it required a full day of traveling by buses. They had to walk at least two hours to get to the first bus stop, and they went through many cities. It was more than a year before I visited them for the first time.

My parents were working hard to keep up with all of us. My oldest brother was between relationships, and as a result—more people were being added to our family.

My siblings and I were going to school to get a basic education and working at home at the same time. Attending school was very difficult since we had to walk far since we were in the middle of three villages. Each of the villages had a school, and some of them only had one teacher. The teachers divided the first and second graders and taught them at the same time. We could go to the one that belonged to our jurisdiction or one that was in another village. Both were far away, and two villages were about four hours away—by foot. We could get our secondary education at those locations. After that, we had to move to a town or a city to finish high school.

Commuting with all those kids was awesome. Even when we didn't have a better way to get to our classrooms, we tried to enjoy the moment by climbing trees and eating whatever we could find. Even those of us who didn't have proper shoes to walk the trails under the heat of the sun never gave up. We could not ride bicycles or use any other mode of transportation because there were no roads. In later years, the community teamed up with the government to begin a road project in the area. Building the road through the hills was almost impossible because of the terrain. We had no equipment or machinery.

My mother's uncle had a big chunk of land and cattle. It was several acres of pasture to tend his cattle, and he used the rest for farming—including sugarcane. He later sold it to a very important man who had in mind to transform that region. That wealthy man was able to get a front loader that helped start the first fifteen kilometers of road. He convinced all the villagers that it was possible to have their dream come true. The landowners agreed that the road would benefit all of us. Armed with picks and shovels, we began to rip through the hill because the machine couldn't do it all since, we only had it for a day or two per week.

That clever man connected with other organizations that helped the poor. Those organizations provided rations for the workers. It was composed of a few pounds of wheat, wheat flour, some pieces of stinking fish, and a can of cooking oil. The ration was the wages for fifteen days of work, and half of the ration was for kids like me.

We started at seven o'clock on the morning and finished at six o'clock in the evening. My father was in charge of the hand drilling and dynamiting big rocks that were in the way. They did it with no training whatsoever. They were just handed a long drill, a slash hammer, and a few sticks of dynamite—and they were ready to go.

The road was to be the supply line for all of us, so we could at least bring our goods to the market and less dependency on our backs, our mules or horses that were the vehicles in use. Now this project was to be worked on during the dry season for that was the time when all the production season for all crops had it come to stop, so we had about for months after we had gathered all our crops and stored them for the following year. That way all men of the village were always doing something, and prior to that road project and even then, there were men who would go to other parts of the country to cotton picking to earn the supplement income, so they could dress themselves and their families.

It was a very exciting time for us as kids. My father used to go to work to a sugar plant while waiting for the next season of crops. My father didn't believe in limitations. The responsibility of feeding and clothing all nine of us didn't matter for him. We didn't own a big piece of land, and our house took up most of the property. There was a separate kitchen with an open corridor that served as an access for the cattle, pigs, and chickens. We also had to keep some open space to feed all the animals and shelter the two horses.

My father had to come up with daily sustenance for his children and all the livestock. He would lease the land where he was going to plant his crops for the year, and from there, he was going to produce everything needed to keep us afloat. We consumed grain, corn, beans of all kinds, and rice. After he picked the crops, he collected all the hay and made sure there was enough for the six months of dry season. When there wasn't enough hay, he would buy it from the neighbors.

Since there were no roads or safe trails for horses to carry out the harvest, there were no machines or tractors to work the land. Everything had to be done by hand—from getting the ground ready to plant the seeds and collecting it. He farmed on two or three locations, and things became complicated. The first crop to be harvested was the beans, and they were yanked from the ground, put in big nets, and carried home. They would be cleaned and stored until the next dry season. The rest was brought to the town market to be sold so we could buy clothes, shoes, and maybe a bit of beef. At home, we had milk, cheese, eggs, and chickens. Sometimes we slaughtered a pig. We had squash, green bananas, and tomatoes. For some reason, none of the villagers produced onion or garlic.

We produced two harvests per season, and the last one included rice, sorghum, beans, and corn. It was hard to collect the grain by hand. The sorghum had to be picked by hand, and none of us wanted to do it. The chaff is so itchy. It is worse than fiberglass. We cut the stems in half, and piled them up until they got completely dry—then we picked the pods, so we could put them in sacks or big nets and hauled them home. It needed to be carried home on our backs, and it was heavy. It was about five kilometers of bad terrain. When my father said we were going to have a great harvest, it didn't make us happy.

After the sorghum was piled up at home, there was a fun part. We had to de-pulp it, and that was the most horrible thing ever. The grain was used to feed the chickens and pigs, and the chaff was for the cattle and horses. When the dry season was longer than expected, my mother used to mix some of the sorghum with the corn. We boiled the corn, added limestone powder, and ran it through a mill or grinder to make tortillas, which were used instead of bread. Our diet was balanced with the natural grains we produced. We had corn tortillas three times a day. For breakfast, instead of eggs and bacon, we had milk straight from the cow. We added the crispy upper layer of the tortilla to make cornflakes.

My sister made feta cheese and served it with thick cream, beans, and hot tortillas, which came straight from the clay pot. A solid breakfast was needed for the day long ahead of us. My father got up first and sharpened his tools. While he was doing that, we had a little extra time to sleep in. One of the sisters prepared breakfast, and other ones prepared everything for lunch, which required time and dedication. They also delivered our lunches. They had to walk for an hour and not be late if they wanted to avoid getting in trouble with my father.

On their way home, they would carry firewood that my father had collected. It was a constant movement that didn't let anyone stand still because there was always something to do. It was hard to keep a balance between work and school. We needed to keep the ball rolling. It was the three brothers and my father, just the two of us, or just my second-oldest brother and my father. I was not counted as full-grown man. I was basically there just to learn farming. My brothers were not very good farmers either.

My oldest brother was twelve years older than me. He had it rough and went to start his own family. My second-oldest brother didn't hang around long enough to learn what it takes to become a true farmer. All the responsibility was on my father's shoulders. This was an enormous task for one man, but my father was a giant. At six feet and few inches tall, he was able to lift more than two hundred pounds and transport it over long distances. He collected all the corn and sorghum for our livestock, and he would get up before sunrise and haul all day long.

Before we brought home the harvest, we prepared a second lot that was big enough to store our production. The lot was one square block, and we had enough room for our horses and a few cows. We de-pulped the sorghum under the shade of a mango and some avocado trees. We used cow dung for the floor. We diluted it in water, turned it into a liquid, and spread it all over the floor. We enclosed the floor with stems from the sorghum or rice hay. We had about four hundred square feet to work on.

Our tools were simple rods that we made from strong trees that grew along the creek. We had to make sure the trees were about four inches in diameter, and they had to be curved up at one end. We thinned them out for good handles. We shaved the bottoms to create a flat surface that was about four inches wide. The length would depend on the height of the person who was going to swing it. Mine was about five feet long and had a long handle for a better impact.

In a good year, we produced twenty or thirty sacks of grain. The sacks weighed two hundred pounds, which means my father transported more than six thousand pounds—almost by himself—including all the chaff. He couldn't have used the horses because the terrain was brutal. The hills were not safe for our horses, and people put up fences for their cattle.

We carried everything on our shoulders, and that included the firewood we collected. We used wood to cook our meals. No firewood meant no food because no one was set up to use other sources of fuel other than kerosene, which was used only for lighting. No one had a kerosene stove or anything else that could be used instead of a wood stove. Therefore, everyone had to be prepared with the fuel needed for every cooking thing. Every household had baking ovens, and they all needed firewood to be heated.

My father was responsible for providing everything for our family. He also had to find time to go to work for someone else. He used to work for a man who had a sugarcane field. In the summer, the ground was hard. He dug holes in the fields so the ground would be ready to plant more sugarcane. The wages for a full day of work were ₡1.50, which was the equivalent of forty cents of a dollar in the seventies. He had it rough, but he never complained. He was on top of everything. If we had a water leak, he wouldn't wait until the next day to fix it. If one or two of our boars were ready to be neutered, he would be ready to act. I have grown old and have never seen such a courageous and determined man.

I have only touched the surface of what my father was in all spheres. I never heard him saying I love you to any of his children, but I know without a doubt that he loved all of us to death. He would rather starve than see his children go hungry. When we were working the fields and sat in the shade for lunch, he would wait until we were satisfied before he ate whatever was left. His philosophy was that none of his children were to go hungry or go to bed with an empty stomach. He would work extra to provide the necessities of life for us.

If he hadn't been the father he was, what would have happened to all of us? How would my mother have been able to raise so many of us since there was no social assistance of any kind. He was left only with the possibility of hard labor to bring home our daily bread. Getting sick never stopped him from getting up and going to work the fields. For him, living in poverty wasn't an option. Rain or shine, he was ready. That courage is the one thing I cannot ignore from the man who practically gave his life to raise me.

A husband without a wife cannot succeed. It is unconceivable not to recognize my mother's figure in the house. She married my father at very young age, and coming from parents who were practically divorced and remarried, she had a great challenge of raising her kids. The wife described in Proverbs 31:10 fits her perfectly. I never knew how she was treated when she was a child, but I am almost certain she was mistreated, and that made her look after her children the way she did.

When I was about ten, she told me how hard the first years of her marriage were. It's hard to believe that my mother would find time to converse with her ten-year-old son about things that probably wouldn't make much sense, but everything happens for a reason. When her first daughter was born, they had nothing. The only thing they had was each other, and they had to thrive because they had the will. She began working to help my father. She knew how to sew, but she had no sewing machine. She had to walk for half an hour to use her friend's machine.

Back then, everybody had to go to town to buy fabric and have their clothes made. My mother specialized in dressmaking and making of men's shirts. She and her friend were responsible for dressing the whole community. They would take turns using the sewing machine, and her friend was taking people from the other end of the village. They had to split the clientele and the machine. I think they each had it for three days a week. In between, she was doing some baking and selling it the village for extra money.

She was charging pennies to make the dresses, and she was gone for the whole day. She came home to get things ready for dinner. A year and a few months separate my oldest sister and my brother. Things started to get more complicated when she had to take care of two instead of one. She had to produce more to get ahead.

After more children, my oldest sister was able to help. She had help in the kitchen and with babysitting since my mom was working double shifts. After she finished her sewing, which was sometimes three or four dresses per day, she would go home to prepare the baking dough for the next day. She had to get up at four o'clock in the morning to have the baking ready at six o'clock. My sister would deliver it around the village. She would come home and carry on with her chores, and my mom would go to her sewing job, which paid her about fifteen to fifty cents, depending on the dress.

We had three major holidays during the year, and the first one was Christmas. In our culture, Christmas is a great deal more than what it is in North America. It is so important that everyone must have new clothes. My mother had to start tailoring in October. It would bring in extra income that was used to buy the fabrics to clothe us. It was a great feeling to be waiting for that big day, and we knew we would be wearing new outfits that Mom had worked so hard on. She always met the deadline for her customers.

Things got easier for Mom as my sisters started getting good at all the things that needed to be done around the house. The responsibility for the house was split among my sisters, and that gave my mom more time to work on the sewing business. She didn't have to worry so much.

For Christmas, everything had to be done from scratch. All our materials were in a raw state, and we produced many different grades of flour. Corn was the main source of most of the products we consumed. There were *tortillas* and *tamales*. A Christmas without *tamales* is not a Christmas in our culture.

For the different breads, the flour had to be processed in different ways with different kinds of grain. The only equipment for this was a grinding stone. When a couple established a home, the first thing to own was the grinding stone that was to be operated by the wife in the kitchen. Beds and tableware were secondary because the women had to create the best dish to feed their families. Since corn was the main ingredient, a mom or a daughter would throw the corn on the grinding stones, which were about twenty by twenty-five inches in diameter and undulated. They would put both hands on a thin, round crusher and roll it just enough to break the grain. This was repeated until they had the dough for *tortillas* or the flour for bread. It was a job for women only. If a man was seen doing that kind of work, it meant he was feminine. He was going to be scorned or called bad names. Everybody was defined by what they did and did not do.

All the work had to be completed by six o'clock on Christmas Eve. I had to get all the firewood to heat up the clay oven two or three times for all the baking that had to be done. The *tamales* were the feature of the night. It was very special night, and the celebration could be heard from far away. There were firecrackers and music from a local band. That night, I got to wear my new clothes and my new shoes. It was not like any other night.

In most parts of the world, children open their presents on Christmas. For us, it was just enough to get up first thing in the morning and get on with the big pot of *tamales* and a home-grown cup of coffee. That was more than a present for us because we got to eat as much bread and sweets as we wanted and hang out with friends and cousins. There was no work or school.

Our joy didn't end at Christmas. December was the best time of the year, and we couldn't ask for anything more between the twenty-fifth and the thirty-first. We stocked up on food and firecrackers because it had to be an unforgettable night. We called Christmas Eve and New Year's Eve *Noche Buena* because everybody was celebrating.

After the two celebrations was the Easter celebration. It was a full week. Men in the fields had to cease all labor, especially with tools. There is a superstition that Christ is being beaten that week. People must be really careful— even when they walk. We had to get everything ready the week before, and we had to collect all the firewood for the entire week.

We were not supposed to swing an axe or a machete because it was considered a sin. There was a belief among the elders that using any tools made you guilty of the death of Christ. As a result, you would be punished. The punishment could be chopping off a hand or another body part.

Tree climbing was also prohibited, and that was one of the hardest things for us because it was our favorite thing to do. We managed to get around it. We thought we were okay if no one saw us. We thought that Jesus was too busy to think of us climbing trees. We tried to keep it a secret from our parents to avoid being punished by them.

The Easter celebration wasn't that fun. It was a time to be sad for what was happening. To be a good person, we had to relive the passion of Christ. As kids, we thought Jesus was being crucified every year, and that gave us more assurance that what our parents were telling us was true. Meat was off the table. No one was supposed to eat meat of any kind because it was like eating Jesus's flesh. Everyone was supposed to go to the market and get the biggest fish because salty, dried fish was supposed to feed us for the whole week.

The preparation of salt cod was the whole key to enjoying every meal. The women were to have everything ready, and feeding nine people with a dried, salted cod wasn't possible. My mother figured it out. She would have spices brought from town or prepare them herself. *Achiote* is native to Central America, and it produces a pod that is the size of a chestnut. It is packed with seeds that are covered with a red pigment. After washing them, we collected the pigment and made a condiment. The boiling water turned into a thick red paste.

After a few hours, we shaped it into small cubes, wrapped it in cornhusks, and tied it with strings made from banana stems. It was organic and had no additives or preservatives. It was used to make the broth and then added to the cod that had it been wrapped in special corn dough. The corn dough was mixed with many ingredients and made into thick circular shapes before putting them in the frying pan. The delicious soup would be served for lunch and dinner, and in the morning, we would have homemade bread and coffee that tasted like no other coffee.

The coffee my mother used to brew and all the pastry were exquisite—and on top of that we would have the cicadas coming up from the ground just in time to sing for Easter. At dusk, they would begin serenading. It was very loud, especially when there were no cars or large crowds. It was amazing to sit under a hut or under a tree and tell stories under a full moon and have the little creatures singing in the background. Some people who were born there go back there to hear the cicadas singing.

Easter was a reflectional time for our community, and for the Christian community, it was even greater celebration. Christians usually pick that week to have their conventions, and the church hosting the event is responsible for feeding all the people. There was no restriction on what people could eat. Some of the ranchers would donate a full-grown cow, and some of the farmers would donate corn, rice, and beans. The women would donate their time. Everybody was involved in the commemoration of the death and resurrection of our Lord.

Some churches would do it within their denomination, and others would be interdenominational. There was a sense of unity among all Christians. I was following traditions at home. My mother was a devoted person of Virgin Mary, and she used to do nine rosaries after a person in the community died. I believed that Easter was when Jews killed Jesus and that we must be submissive because the earth was hurting that week. After Easter Sunday, we could run, jump, ride horses, and climb trees. It felt good to pause for that time even though we didn't understand the story of Jesus. My mother and my grandparents tried to teach what they knew, but it was not enough because they also needed to be rescued.

My childhood was full of good and bad memories, and going back there makes me think about how hard it was for my parents to raise nine of us in such primitive conditions. My father—equipped with just a *machete* and few handmade tools—was able to give us the basics of life. His wife stood beside him, and she never neglected her responsibilities to her children. Instead, she went beyond what a person needs to do. Equipped with just the knowledge of a housewife and the will to thrive for the survival of her children, she was capable of giving us her love and complete devotion. That wife was my mother.

CHAPTER 2

My Parents' Conversion and the Day My Father Explained Revelations 9

So then faith cometh by hearing, and
hearing by the Word of God.

—Romans 10:17

My father was born into the traditional religion of Central America. He was raised Catholic, and there was no hope from his parents or siblings that they would influence him to become a Christian. They embraced Catholicism until death, for that was their inheritance left from their ancestors, and to change that was to betray their family and religion. I did see families being divided or family members mistreated because they decided to become Christians. However, the Gospel made a breakthrough into my village, and it came to the village through one of my father's cousins who had been saved in a different country. When he came back, he came as a pastor. His family faced great opposition from the whole village. Without wasting any time, he started a church in his father's house. He miraculously was saved soon after his son's arrival, although he didn't want anything to do with the so-called protestants.

The opposition continued growing stronger, and some of the villagers ambushed the Christians and stoned them. They chanted, "We don't want any Protestants in our village." There was one occasion when one of the pastor's relatives blew up dynamite behind the house where the pastor was preaching. They would barricade the roads with thorny branches to make it miserable for the so-called Protestants. The services were at night in a village where there were no police or electricity. The only lighting was lanterns or flashlights.

Regardless of the constant tormenting of the locals who called themselves enemies of the Gospel, people were being saved. A group got together and ambushed the Christians who were coming from a service in another village. It was dark, and the pastor and the people with him were walking under a lantern. They were attacked with *machetes* and stones. Christians men stood up and put up a fight. One of the brothers was badly injured while he was disarming one of the men with a *machete*.

The man defending the Christians was about to lose a

few fingers, but he recovered from his injuries. There were no police to report the incidents since there wasn't a police station nearby. I believe the Lord used this incident to put a stop to the people who were trying to stop the work the pastor was doing in the community. After that incident, the people started to come to the Lord. Three of my sisters were attending the meetings, and they connected with the idea of a new religion. Soon after, they were saved. A great revival shook the region, including villages that were far away from where the real action was happening.

It didn't take long for my father to start thinking that something different had come to the village. If it was God, he had to find it for himself. He looked in a Catholic Bible to find out the source of whatever had touched his three daughters. My father spent a lot of time reading his Bible under the shade of a mango tree. He had no desire to go to Mass until he knew the truth about God. On Sundays, he would read the scriptures. During the week, there was not enough time to read books or to go to Bible studies because the workload was enormous. He would find time to read the Bible, but it produced more question than answers. That left him no choice but to welcome the pastor. The pastor told him about God.

When my sisters were baptized, my father found delight in the new religion. He told his parents that he was going to change his religion. I wasn't there when it happened, but I know it wasn't easy for them to hear that he was renouncing their religion. My grandparents believed that my father was changing his religion and damning himself by becoming a Protestant.

My father and mother decided to attend meetings at the pastor's house since there was no church yet. The services were being held in people's homes during the week. On Sundays, they were at the pastor's home under a tent made from reeds. We had a few chairs and a small table as a pulpit on a dirt floor. Sunday services were held in the afternoon.

People enjoyed life and tried to serve God and serve people. My father and my mother connected to that way of living since they saw something different from what they had known all along. It didn't take long before they connected to the new group of believers. They began to learn a new way of living. They had been struggling with smoking for many years, and they were ready to quit for good. They had to fight the addiction to smoking cigarettes—and not just any cigarettes, but the ones they made themselves. Determined that nothing was going to stop them from following Jesus, they began a journey to the unknown trusting that they were not alone. Confident that this time they were not going to fail to stop smoking, they went forward.

They were ready to face the consequences, but hey had discovered something greater than anything they had ever known. They continued struggling with their addiction and trying to hide it from the other believers. Since smoking is not something that anyone can simply hide, they were confronted with reality. They were forced to pray harder and put their faith in action. They were ready to show whoever knew them that they could leave everything behind for the sake of Jesus. He was going to back them up.

As a teen, I was able to see more of their struggle. My father had terrible headaches every time he tried to quit. My mother was in worse shape. She was in charge of making the cigarettes, and I was in charge of finding the best tobacco so she could roast it and roll the cigarettes. Sometimes I had to go to two or three different places if they were not pleased with it. Some of the tobacco was imported from other countries in bundles of dried leaves. My mother would have to crush it after putting it in a pot to roast it. The pastor said they were supposed to come clean because the Bible says, "If anyone is in Christ is a new creation and the old things are passed away." There were times they were not greeted as Christians because they hadn't been able to overcome that addiction. Thankfully, this attitude didn't keep them from pursuing their dream to become accepted by Christ Jesus and accepted in the church.

They asked the pastor to be baptized, but they had to quit smoking for him to baptize them. They had committed to never smoke again. They were put on trial until the pastor could see if they were completely free from the addiction. They reached for something from out of this world because there was no way they could do it alone. There had to be a divine intervention for it to become a reality in their lives. God showed Himself to them. I saw a total transformation.

My mother had a condition that no doctor had been able to diagnose. She suffered from a pain that would put her near the brink of death. It was horrendous to see my mother clinging to life, surrounded by her kids, and unable to do anything. Neighbors and my grandma tried to revive her by putting spirits on her nose and breathing them in. The pain would attack her chest and go up her throat. It felt like someone was choking her. She had been suffering a satanic attack, and no one could do anything about it.

The doctor reports showed that she was in an excellent health, and there was no explanation for the episodes. One time, all of us were crying because she wouldn't respond for at least five minutes. She was dead. My father mixed a bottle of alcohol—the only medicine available—with water to try to revive her. He was trying anything to save his wife.

My mother came back to life after sorrow had filled the house. We all began crying tears of joy. Besides her body aching from the struggle, she didn't remember anything. Everything was normal for her, and she carried on with her routine. I'm sure it wasn't an epileptic attack or seizure because she had been tested for all of those possibilities. It had to be something else. "So if the Son sets you free, you will be free indeed." The Lord was waiting for my mother to fully trust Him, so He could begin to set her free.

Their trial had come to an end, and they were ready for baptism. As they were going down to the waters, the first miracle happened for my mother. When she came out of the water, she was a new creation—and so was my father. The Lord had taken away the smoking addiction from both of them, and He had set my mother free from the demon that had been tormenting her for years. She started living a completely different life physically and spiritually. Without a doubt, the miracles impacted all those who were familiar with our situation. Even our grandparents stood back and no longer harassed them because they had become Protestants.

My parents began a new journey where all things were possible. They were witnesses of the transforming power of Jesus. There was no way they would have been able to have that total transformation on their own and experienced the power of healing. It was like a dream for my mother and father. The scriptures had come alive. They had seen the power of God, and it was something they had contemplated with their own eyes. The Gospel had made its way to our house. It had started with my sisters, and my parents joined them. Church was coming home. My father opened the doors, and services began happening. Although we didn't have a big house to accommodate a large crowd of people, we had a big patio. The church lantern began to shine, and the Gospel continued to be preached. People continued to be saved.

The promise of God had come to my house while I was still in the process of becoming a grown-up man. Grace had found its way into our home even though we had done nothing to deserve it. God wanted to bring His light into our lives so we could carry others to His path. From that day forward, we were called Evangelicals. Even though I was just a kid, people saw me as one of "them." Perhaps my father didn't fully grasp that people were going to treat him differently—and he was supposed to love them in return.

I was going home from school with my sister and my friend. We decided to stop by where one of the villagers was processing the sugarcane into some sort of candy that was used in most parts of the country to sweeten the coffee. It is derived from the sugarcane while it is processed. It was common for parents to let their kids to go to these places for sugary treats. It was normal for us to stop and enjoy all that sweet stuff.

The man who owned the place told me to leave his property. He knew my father was a Christian, and he hated people who were Protestants. He picked me out from all the kids and told me that I was not to go back to his place because he didn't like us. No one had ever said hateful things like that to me. I was rejected for something that didn't make any sense to me. I knew it was not going to go well with my father. My mother kept it from him. I think she told him later that year. My father knew there was a price to pay for the sake of Jesus, and he accepted that there was a different battle to fight from then on.

The years went by, and my father started to get involved in church. There was not a building we could call a church, but we were happy to know that God was present at all our meetings and that soon we were going to build our church. The Lord began to bless our home. My father could afford to hire workers to help with the work, and I was blessed as well. I did less farming and dedicated more time to taking care of the livestock. If I had school on the morning, I had to go home and carry on with my endless chores.

My father was concerned that I was in my teen years and had not decided to follow Christ. Through his rough character, I begin to see his tenderness toward me. I was his favorite son because I was his last son. I couldn't make it up at the time. I was young, and it took more for me to see those things. My brothers were gone, and my father was going to do whatever it took to keep me around. I was the next in line to pick it up after him.

My mother noticed that he was favoring me over everyone else. I heard them arguing about it, and I tried to manipulate things for my own gain. My sisters were busy with their own things, and most of them had left home. Some started families of their own, and others worked in the city like my brothers. I was alone, and I felt oppressed. I wanted to explore and find out for myself what it was like to leave home and live under my own rules. I wasn't even allowed to go to the city by myself because my father was afraid something bad would happen to me.

At fourteen, I had not even been to a beach or any other place where kids would normally go. It was common for people to go on vacation during Easter week. I made big plans with my friends to go to fairs in towns near us, but my father wouldn't let me go. I never went on a ride because for my father thought it was too dangerous. I wanted to know what it felt like to be free and do things other kids did. The first time I went on a ride was when I was fifteen, and it happened because I was chaperoning one of my sisters. As a bribe, she let me go on a ride—and her boyfriend paid for the ride.

I was faced with the reality of another world, which I wasn't looking for. I just started to wake up to the world my friends were living in. I wanted to be part of that world. I was sneaking out to the soccer field with my friends to play or watch a game while my father was at church. It was a big temptation for me. The soccer field was just a block away from my house, and every Sunday, there was a big game with the local team. I had to be there with my friends—even with the disapproval of my father. My father was against me going to places like that because there people were drinking, gambling, smoking, and using obscene language. My father wanted to protect me from getting mixed up with that kind of people and keep me from getting hurt. Where there is gambling and alcohol, there always will be trouble.

I had witnessed so many bad things, but that didn't deter me from getting out there and living in the moment of excitement with the soccer fans. My oldest brother was the goalkeeper, and I felt like I needed to be there cheering for my team. That wasn't the case for my father. He always was on the lookout to make sure I didn't disappear on Sundays during soccer season. He would do anything to prevent me from going to the games. My only chance to escape was when he was at the church and I had finished my chores. In my mind, there was no church for me. I had attended to a few Sunday school sessions, but my mind was captivated by the power of the things of the world. My father never gave up on me.

On a hot autumn afternoon, my father called me to the shade of a wild almond tree. We were getting one of the fields we had leased ready for the corn and beans, and he told me to take a break. I saw something in my father I had never seen before. His personality transformed, and I didn't know what was going on or what was going to happen. He asked me to sit beside him, and I did. A *tecomate* is a natural jar to keep drinking water cool. He talked to me in a way that he never had talked to me before. He started opening his heart to me under that tree, and I knew he was expressing love and trying to tell me something important.

The Holy Spirit sowed the seed of the Gospel in me

through my father. Being a rough man with no special training or theological knowledge other than his time alone with his Bible, I knew the Holy Spirit was talking through him. He began reciting Revelations 9. He said, "Son I want to tell you what is coming to this earth."

When he started verse 1, I could see the star coming from heaven to earth and opening the bottomless pit. I could see all the horrible creatures preparing to hurt mankind, and the thing that struck me the most was that they were tormenting those who didn't have the seal of God. I thought I needed that seal to be protected. As my father carried on, I was more intrigued and wanted to know more. I didn't have a Bible, and we were not allowed to touch my father's Bible. Perhaps it was a mistake not to provide the Holy Book for each of us, but that practice wasn't common in his era. Besides that, buying each of us a Bible would be too much for a man whose earnings were forty cents for a full day's work.

As he continued narrating, I was glued to a rock. I listened about all the beasts stinging mankind. It kind of made sense that they were not hurting the trees since I was sitting under a beautiful tree. I visualized how it would be if these strange characters were to destroy all vegetation. The way he described them was horrendous. Since there was no place to hide, I imagined them coming toward me. The only way I could be saved was if I had the seal of God.

I didn't know how to get out of the situation or how to

get the stamp that would prevent them from hurting me. They were so real in my mind. I could almost see their faces, long hair, and lion's teeth. It was awful.

He said, "And in those days men shall seek death but death shall hide from them. Men will want to die instead of live."

That was even more terrifying than seeing people running and hitting themselves or cutting themselves. I pictured the person of death running away from people because she didn't want to kill anyone. It was a grim picture I had seen in my mind, and I was speechless.

My father never asked if I wanted to receive Jesus in my heart. He never told me that doing so would give me the seal the scripture was talking about. I'm sure he didn't ask me to receive the Lord because he didn't know how. He was new in faith and had no idea how to walk someone to the Lord. He was sure I was under a promise and that I was going to become a Christian. God would send someone else who was more qualified to explain the Gospel.

The break was over, but I knew my father had to have an encounter with something. We went home, and I carried on with my normal routine. Something had changed in me. I was not crazy about it, but every time I thought in the way I used to, I thought about the conversation with my father. I saw myself facing the consequences like the people in the picture my father had painted for me.

I would try to have fun like the other teenagers, but I

was embarrassed when I thought about what my father would have done to me if he knew what I was doing behind his back. The other teenagers had no problem with that because none of their parents were associated with the Gospel or went to church. Ever since that conversation with my father, I found myself standing between two roads. The desire to be like my friends was pulling me in one direction, and something else was pulling me into it. I knew that it was good. I didn't know if it was because I had seen the future of those who disobeyed God or because God was preserving me for something better.

My father wasn't trying to scare me or make me believe in what he believed. He had shown something different that wasn't within his reach. Somehow, he managed to break off from his harsh character. He was trying to reach out to me, and it was beyond his ability to communicate the kingdom of God. He loved me, but he didn't know how to show it.

Revelations 9 played a big part in my conversion to Christianity, and I have no doubt God used my father to imprint His holy fear in me so I could repent for His glory. It doesn't matter how and where. It was done in the humblest way, but it was effective because listening my father being used by the Holy Spirit showed me the separation between good and evil. When humanity is afflicted with pain and sorrow, there is nothing more important that will give us peace or make us free.

I didn't fully comprehend the spectrum of salvation,

but it brought me the conviction of the existence of God, which I couldn't run away from. I hadn't confessed to Him yet as Lord and Savior, but He had already marked my heart with His Word. My decision was because I had seen humankind's future. I had seen the future of those who lived their lives for themselves apart from God. They didn't take Him into account, and they were excluded from the possibility of living with our heavenly Father forever.

CHAPTER 3

The Night the Lord Saved Me

Before I formed thee in the belly I knew
thee. And before thou camest forth out of
the womb I sanctified thee, and I ordained
thee a prophet unto the nations.

I continued living my life as normally as any teenager
would, although for the rest of the other kids, I wasn't
normal because I couldn't do the things they did. I tried
to fit in and be part of their world. I had forgotten about
that experience that brought me closeness with God and
began to sneak out.

I went to a few school dances, and my parents didn't
pay much attention to it because it was part of the school
curriculum. It wasn't in my best interests to let them
know what was going on at school. Parents relied on the

system, and some of them had no idea what was going on at school. Buying the textbooks and other school supplies for their kids was their entire involvement.

Teachers used to go around the village to register the kids for school. Sometimes they had to fight with parents to let their kids go to school. I was playing soccer and baseball at school. Our team played against teams from other jurisdictions, and it was fun because we traveled to other schools with the girls' baseball team. It was awesome to go up and down the hills and go back to our school. Whether victorious or not, our teachers gave it all for the sake of the students. Sometimes the teachers had to invest from their miserable salaries to accommodate the needs of their students—without expecting to get anything in return. They just wanted to give us a chance to have a good time.

The other kids went home and shared the game with their fathers. I went home and acted like I had never left the classroom. My father wouldn't approve of his son being anywhere that wasn't school. It was always in the back of my mind that my father didn't know when we were going to those activities. He thought those activities were associated with vandalism and bad influences. I had no choice but to pretend I was a good boy and that I was behaving the same way as I did at home. My fear was that my father would show up to one of these games and see me. He would have pulled me out in front of everybody, and he had done it before. I couldn't bear the embarrassment, especially if he were to do it in front the girls. I did not want my classmates and friends making fun of me. It only happened a few times, but God had mercy on me. It only happened in front of the boys on the soccer field near my home. I'm sure he wanted to protect me from a lifestyle that wasn't one he wanted for his son. He had seen the results of that environment, and they were not good. He tried to divert me from those he thought were not suitable, and he managed to keep me away until the age of fourteen.

There was not much time for me to experience everything the world had to offer. I had no time to get drunk, get high on drugs, be addicted to smoking, or try any kind of gambling. I could not even play a game of cards because that was considered bad in the eyes of my father. Because of his discipline, I was able to escape from the claws of the devil. Most of my friends didn't make it. Some of them did not even make it to the age of thirty. They got caught up in the life I thought it was cool, and others were killed during the brutal civil war that struck my country during the eighties. I don't regret for a moment that I wasn't able to be part of those who believed I was being oppressed by my father's rules since I couldn't join their crowds. They were doing everything against the creed, and it seemed ridiculous to me. I believe God sent His angel to watch over me, and because of that, I am still telling the story.

In October, just a month before my fifteenth birthday,

my mother asked me to accompany her to church. We had just finished bringing inside all the beans that had drying on the patio during the day. The beans were still on the chaff, and we bundled them up until they were crisp and dry. After drying the beans, we beat them with a rod to clean them. After we moved the bundles inside, we had to go through the whole area and pick up all the beans that had fallen out of the pods. We had done that with some of my sisters, and we were happy to have the place clear to play. My mom interrupted and asked me to go to church with her. The church was about twenty minutes walking, and the services started at seven. It was already dark, and there were not even roads for the most part. We had to get a flashlight or lantern, and the trails climbed up hills. I didn't want to go to this meeting because it was going to be boring, and I was going to miss all the fun at the house. We had everything set up to play our games. I asked, "Why me?"

My mother said, "Because I'm asking you."

I was left with not much of a choice but to get ready and start walking to the church meeting. It didn't take long to get there, and the meeting had already started when we arrived. To be honest, there was nothing exciting going on. For my mother, that was okay because she used to do dead people's prayers, but for me, it was a torment being there. Nothing made sense to me. I was somewhat terrified. I sat behind a pillar in the middle of the room.

Most of the people were old, and most of them were

our relatives. Therefore, there was no respect for the little guy. They were making sure I didn't look for a corner to sleep in until the service was over. To make matters worse, there was no music of any kind. Our family loved music, and the village band was composed in part by some of the people in that room—beginning with the pastor. They didn't believe music was good in church, and they got the idea that music was no good because it exalts the flesh and not the spirit.

They didn't even clap because it was not appropriate in the service. The pastor greeted everybody and said, "We are glad for our little friend who has decided to join us tonight." He went on and on like I really was there by my own will. He began preaching for more than an hour, and I was wondering when he was going to finish. I didn't really know what his message was about. I wasn't paying any attention. All I wanted was to go home and be surrounded by the other kids who were playing all the fun games we used to play. The sermon came to an end, and he began an altar call for "those who want to receive Jesus as their Lord and Savior."

I was the only one there who needed a Savior. It was the most important moment of my life, and it has been highlighted throughout my life. When you are looking for nothing, and someone hands you a million dollars—you don't want to take it because you think no one gives nothing for nothing. What is being given doesn't interest you or is totally fake.

The pastor carried on with the altar call, and I moved behind the pillar. I felt a sense of protection since he couldn't see my face. As he called me directly, my knees began to shake. I felt like a magnetic force was pulling me toward the pulpit. I tried to hold on as hard as I could, but my strength had left me. I didn't know what to do.

I didn't know if I should hate my mom or leave home. I never wanted to go through that again. I managed to survive that episode.

The pastor said, "For your next visit, maybe you will make a decision to receive Christ as your Lord and savior." He turned to his assistant and closed the service. When I heard those words, I was relieved. The pressure that had been pulling on me was gone. I sat on a bench without saying a word.

I thought the night was over, but there was another sermon yet to be preached. Shortly after I sat down, the assistant pastor got up and started to recapitulate the sermon. It was a second sermon, and I had no say in the matter. It never occurred me that he was going to carry on with the altar call. He went straight to me and said, "Young man, today is your day of salvation." I don't remember if I looked around to see who was looking or if I looked at the floor, but I was more scared than before. A sense of fear came over me, and I didn't know what to do. The man was insisting that I step forward to receive Christ. I was not supposed to leave without Him.

It's not normal to push people to come to the front

and try to save them by force, but back in those days, they didn't know any better—since the Scriptures says, "Strive to enter in at the strait gate" (Luke 13:24 KJV). They thought they had to push people to enter the kingdom of heaven. Otherwise, they were not preaching the Gospel the right way.

He had a real heart for Jesus. I could see he was calling me to true happiness. I could see his face glowing, and he was smiling like he was seeing Jesus at the same time he was calling me to the altar. My fears went away, and I thought, *What about my friends? What will I tell them if I turn myself to Jesus? Will they understand me and still be my friends? I am about to turn fifteen, and I want to bury myself with these halleluiah people?*

I tried to hide behind the pillar, but the current was too strong. My legs were shaking, and before I realized it, I was in front of the pillar, facing the preacher. I was no longer in control. The current was like a rushing river dragging everything in its path, and I was trying to hold on to something I didn't have to hold on to. It seemed like a nightmare. I wanted to wake up, carry on with my life, and follow my own desires. The current took me right to the altar. The preacher was telling me how much Jesus loved me and that he was going to pray for me.

Everybody shouted, "Hallelujah! Praise the Lord"

As I was about to pray the sinner's prayer, a thought came to my mind. A little voice said, "If you do this, you will lose all the fun. You'll be dead!"

The church was praying I would decide to follow Christ, but I still wasn't fully convinced that it was my own desire to be in that place. If I could fake it, it was going to be all right since no one would be able to tell whether I was being truthful in my decision to accept Christ. The dilemma in my mind went on for a few minutes, but the church's prayer was finally heard. I was free to claim Christ as my Lord and Savior.

Before I knew it, I was praying the sinner's prayer in front of everybody. Something that I wasn't planning on doing had happened. All people who were present were witnesses that I had become a Christian, and I had no place to hide. They were going to be everywhere, and doing anything wrong would be enough to lose the Christian title.

My mother was happier than I was that her son had become a Christian, but I wasn't happy. I had to invent something to tell my friends. That didn't sound too compromising since I still needed them. With that decision came the scorn of all those who weren't Christians. I was going to be called names by those who hated Christianity, and I wasn't ready for that. My only support was from those in that room, and they were not many. I didn't know the whole of heaven was behind my decision.

The preacher was celebrating for me, and he reassured me that the angels in heaven were also celebrating for me. That brought me a little comfort, but my heart wasn't fully convinced about all the wonderful things these Christians were saying about what it meant to be a Christian. I was about to go on a journey to find out for myself what those people were talking about.

The services concluded, and everybody was congratulating me for a great decision. I looked around, and there were no young people other than the preacher's beautiful daughter. Liuna was the same age as me. She was watching me, but I think she was too afraid to congratulate me.

My journey began, but that night, I had enough. The way home had never seemed as far as that night. My mother was silent all the way home. I was trying to determine my next move, and the little voice in my head said, "You're dead—and now you can't have fun."

I had to come up with a solution to tell my friends why I was not going to sneak out to play with them anymore. I wasn't concerned about being rejected by them. I was concerned about being mocked at school. I thought about what I was going to do when they asked me to join them in a soccer game. I couldn't tell them that I was not going to play soccer because I was a Christian now. How was I supposed to explain that to a big number of people? How would I respond on weekends when the whole village poured down to the soccer field to watch the games? They all knew I liked to be there watching the games.

I would be a subject of mockery for all those people! I thought the solution was to tell some of my friends—in the form of a joke—that I had become a Christian and wasn't going to be touching the ball because it was a sin. I knew they were going to laugh about it, but that was okay because the plan was not to take it seriously. That would buy me time while the news that I had become a Christian spread throughout the village. When I say Christian, I can't use the names related to what those people used to call the Evangelical community other than "Hallelujah" or "Protestant." Catholicism was ingrained in their minds, and they were going to defend it at all costs.

My plan looked like it was going to work. It would give me a chance to change my mind later if I was caught doing something bad. If I was confronted by the people who had witnessed my confession of faith, I would say it was just a joke.

In the morning, everything should be forgotten. If not, I was going to carry on with the original plan. When I woke up, I thought, *My God—what have I done?*

The Holy Spirit took control of the situation. I was not alone. Reinforcements had come from heaven and would make things better. I was compelled to look for a corner to pray. I began to comprehend that someone divine was with me in that room. That person started to talk to my spirit in a voice a fourteen-year-old could understand. The voice said, "What if—instead of falsifying Christianity— you become genuine so all those you call friends can see the real Christians?"

Down on my knees between a wall and my older sister's bed, I said, "I am here to be different so these people can see you, Jesus." I didn't have better words than those, but I knew the Holy Spirit was there with me. He was showing me a picture of my future Christian life. I saw myself preaching the Gospel to a large crowd and being transformed into a new person. I kept on listening.

"You will be different than everybody else."

I saw myself as a young man empowered by the Holy Spirit. I was speaking boldly to the crowds, and none of those people mocked me or made fun of me. Everybody were listening, and I was there to make a difference among those who needed the Gospel. I was being born into a new person. All my fears were gone without even knowing the scriptures. I knew I was going to speak to others about the love of God through Jesus. My mind was completely changed. I didn't care whether I had friends or not. The power of the Holy Spirit was being manifested in front of me through that vision. He was taking over my life and moving in with me. I was being taken to make a difference among those I related with and with my sibling and relatives.

When I finished that moment in the presence of God, I lifted my hands, thanked God, and promised I was there to be different from everyone else. I hadn't realized my sister was still on the bed and had listened to my prayer. When I finished praying, she started laughing. I didn't care because I had been in the presence of God. From that day on, my life was changed. I had been trying to close my heart to the call of the night before, thinking it wasn't my time yet. I tried to ignore the fact that the Lord had been preparing me since before I was born.

My father had tried to protect me and keep me away from any wrongdoing. My heart was blind to the fact that the Lord had appointed all those people to stand fearlessly on the path of righteousness so I could get to my appointed destination. Their encouragement didn't work until I had that personal encounter with my Creator. He decided to send His Holy Spirit to help me break loose from the chains of sin that were keeping me from escaping to the freedom He was offering me. That freedom became real to me when the Holy Spirit engulfed me with His presence, and it was only until then that I managed to break free.

If the Son set you free, you shall be free indeed. I was on the road to prove who Jesus was. I had received that from the Holy Spirit when He helped me break free from the prison I had been locked in. I could see others in great need of Christ, and I was being given the command to go and demonstrate the real Gospel through my living testimony. I received the command to go, and I was empowered to witness others within hours of my encounter with Jesus. I was able to stand up to the haters and preach to them. I acquired a Bible, and it didn't take long before I fell in love with it. I read from Genesis right through Revelations. I was absorbing everything I could. I memorized enough material to provide witness to others.

It's impressive what the Lord can do when we say, "Yes, Lord. Here I am."

I was as a teenager, and God was using me to telling people about the love of Jesus. The first Bible verse I memorized was John 3:16, and being the center of the scriptures, it was all I needed to communicate the love of the Father. God put me there to witness the most difficult people in the village, beginning with my grandparents. They were enemies of the Gospel, and the last thing they wanted to hear was me going to their house and witnessing to them. I used to stand with boldness and explain that there was no place in heaven for idolaters, and they didn't like it. They were filled with deep resentment for my father changing his religion, and then I was trying to bring them to meet Jesus. They were angry and asked me to not to interfere in their lives. They were going to die in their religion, and my uncles and aunts were also against me. I had no trouble letting them know there is no salvation to men unless through Jesus.

For my greatest joy, eight years later I returned to see my grandpa after learning that my grandma had passed away. Both of them had been saved. They were staying with one of my uncles who also had been saved, and he assisted my grandma in her final moments. He had the opportunity to ask if she wanted to receive Jesus. She was able to nod her head yes since she couldn't talk anymore. My uncle had the privilege to walk her through the gates of heaven, and as he finished praying, she squeezed his hand in confirmation that she had received Christ. She took her final breath and went with Jesus.

I had the privilege to pray with my grandpa for the first time. Unfortunately, it was my first and last opportunity to pray with him before he passed away. I thank Christ for allowing me to reap the fruit of my labor. I never thought I would be praying in the same room with him. My heart was overwhelmed in that moment. The Lord brought to my mind back to the days when I was preaching to him. He was so stubborn that he didn't want anything to do with the Evangelical community. Unfortunately, one of my uncles had passed away while rejecting "the Protestant religion." He never wanted to listen to any of us when we tried to share the Gospel with him. He said that he had been born Catholic, and he was going to die Catholic.

It was amazing to see my grandpa saved since he didn't want to change his religion and had said that he was going to die Catholic. I knew I had accomplished my mission. My grandpa had experienced the transforming power of Jesus at the age of eighty-five. He was able to quit chewing tobacco and let the people he despised—Protestants— minister to him instead.

We gathered in my uncle's house for a day, and I kind of knew it was my last time with him. I tried to get the most of that moment. I had to return to Canada, and it was hard to say goodbye since I had spent my childhood so close to him. I can't say I was his favorite grandchild because there were so many of us, but he was there to help in any way he could.

One night when my father wasn't home, my mom was alone with some of us. A drunk man came to our house and wanted to come in. All of us were so afraid of the man. She was more concerned for my sisters. Since the man was armed with a *machete* and the door wasn't safe enough to hold the man out, we were in bad shape. I was about seven, and my brother was about eleven. We wanted to take the man down with our slingshots, but my mom didn't let us go out. The man spent half an hour trying to break in. My grandpa lived half a block away. When the man was about to break in, my grandpa showed up with a big rod that he used to hold his front door closed. With the rod in his hands, he told the man to leave immediately—or he was not going to live to see another day. The man tried to put up a fight but soon realized he was no match for my grandpa.

On the last day I spent with my grandpa, we held hands with some of my cousins in a circle and prayed to Jesus. Even though we were not sure to see each other again on earth, we were certain to see each other in the kingdom of heaven. It wasn't easy to say goodbye to my grandpa, especially when I knew it was the last time I was going to see him alive. The bittersweet news came a few years later that he had passed away. I was glad he had gone to meet his Maker, but part of me was sad that I was not going to see the man who had been my training field. He was one of the first people of my ministry who the Lord had put in my path to bring the good news of the kingdom of heaven.

The night I said yes to the Lord Christ Jesus was written in heaven. Although it didn't make much sense to me, it did for the Lord. Although I was not thinking about the long term, He had me marked for His service. I tried to avoid His calling, but He gave me an opportunity to meet Him personally. Even when I tried to hide from Him, He knew exactly where I was standing. He gave me a chance to get to know Him. Even when I had no strength to follow through, He was quick to send me the Holy Spirit to give me guidance so I wouldn't face the world alone.

In His book, it was written that I was going to produce more children for His kingdom. I had the honor to witness many people, and they were impacted by the words the Holy Spirit put in my mouth for them. One of my uncles tried to stop me from being baptized. He told me obscenities about the pastor, and he tried to pull me away from the baptism.

Eight years later, he was lining up to be baptized by the same pastor who had baptized me. His Word is true, I have lived to see the end of the mockers who tried to be rocks in my path. I have seen my merciful Father bringing them to repentance as He did with me.

CHAPTER 4

At the Baptismal Pool

And he said unto them, Go ye into all the world,
and preach the gospel to every creature. He
that believeth and is baptized shall be saved.
But he that believeth not shall be damned.

—Mark 16:15–16

Seven months after my encounter with Christ, I had to make a decision to be baptized. Baptism was something that came naturally for me. The second set of verses I learned were Mark 16:15 and Mark 16:16. They became real for me, and I was not going to take a chance of neglecting that great commandment.

I felt incomplete, and I had to be baptized as soon as possible to be qualified to enter the kingdom of heaven. In my mind, if I was to die or if Christ appeared to take

His church, I wasn't going to make it to heaven. The Bible says, "Whoever believes and is baptized." I was not going to take any chances of missing or gambling with my salvation. I had to be ready to board the ship of the Gospel, and baptism was my ticket. As long as I had it, I was going to be all right.

My parents were kind of surprised by my decision and asked if it was what I wanted or if the pastor had something to do with it. My response was even more surprising to them. My father sat down with me and explained what baptism meant. If I was sure it was what I wanted, it was okay with him as well. My mother was happy to see her son go one step further in obedience, and the only thing she said was that baptism wasn't a game. I must keep myself for the Lord and be an example to others.

Right after that, Mom and I went to communicate the news to the pastor that I wanted to be baptized. The pastor was more excited than my parents and began to set up things with his people so they could perform that wonderful event. It was such a great deal for me. To begin with, we had to wait until the winter when we had water in the creeks. In the spring, we would get a few light storms, but it wasn't enough to clean and leave a pool that was deep enough to go into. We had no other choice since water is scarce to that region. The women had to fetch the drinking and cooking water, and they had to walk about half an hour just to get a bucket of water. In the summer, everyone struggles for water. There are no pools to submerge anyone.

We had to depend on the weather and hope for a lot of rain to fill the creeks. It was a big job to get things ready. We had to wait for the right time, and all the men of the church would go down the creek to make a temporary pool with branches, rocks, and sand. The pool had to be deep enough for at least three people at the time. I had helped with building numerous pools. It was very cool for the kids. We enjoyed the nice, clean pool after every baptism. After we completed the project, someone had to watch over the pool. There were people who hated us, and they didn't have any problems with destroying our pools.

On Sunday morning, the pastor led a group of volunteers up to dig the pool. After hours of work, the pastor had to go back to get ready. We had to be on the lookout because it was the route for people on horses, and we had no way of telling those coming from other villages that the road was going to be blocked. The event lasted the whole day, which made people mad. There were a number of unhappy people, but the baptism was the greatest thing of all. None of the haters dared to do anything to prevent the event from happening.

We told them we were having baptisms, and that was it. The creek was public, but there was no municipality controlling it. We had no way of getting a permit or anything that gave us security. Only the grace of God was on our side. There were no police of any kind to rely on for protection. The closest police station was about two hours away on horseback. We relied on God's protection and trusted that everything was going to go according to plan.

Baptism had a deep meaning. It wasn't like going to the public swimming pool, taking a dive, and coming out on the other side feeling the same way as we went in. Baptism had a more profound meaning for us. We had an expectation that a new person was coming out of those waters, and even the unbelievers had that concept from people being baptized. They expected a person who had gone through the process of baptism to be totally different person. Perhaps they wanted to see how genuine a person was—or they just wanted to see how they could take advantage of that person. We had made a commitment to serve God, and they thought we were going to be easy prey for them. It was easy for them to point fingers when a believer made a mistake. That constant pressure helped us seek perfection through Jesus Christ.

The event took place before the eyes of the whole village on a Sunday by the soccer field. Everybody congregated to play soccer, drink, and gamble. I believe Jesus was pleased to watch a handful of people doing what He once did. He felt the same pressure, and we have no excuses. It was a great way to preach the Gospel, and that was one of the reasons we didn't do it differently. If Jesus did it publicly, we would bear the responsibility to do it in public too.

None of that could make me stand back from my decision. I made up my mind that I needed to be baptized because I wanted to be right with God. The Holy Spirit had convinced me that there was nothing else in this world for me to go to. He convinced me that I was only to go forward and not backward and that all I needed was in Him.

He had fulfilled every need in me, and I should not want anything. I believed Him. My friends and relatives heard I was going to be baptized and thought I was crazy and was going to be buried alive. I was young, and I was not going to enjoy the pleasures of this world. At the age of fifteen they thought I was too young and foolish to give up my "youth."

None of my sisters were going to church at the time. Perhaps they thought it was just a simple emotion that would go away soon. They thought I had no clue about what I was getting into. I think they could relate that feeling. They tried to serve God, but the pressures of the world put off their desire. I had no encouragement from them or my brothers. My brothers used to mock me. For my relatives, I was a kid with strange ideas. They thought I was trying to convert everyone to become like me.

For other people, I was just a kid. They didn't know there was a fire inside me that couldn't be put out. I had my mind set up to the highest point, and I was not going to change it. My pleasure was to dig into the Word of God and hear the voice of the Holy Spirit telling me that every word I read was true. I was going to be able to do the things that Jesus did. I began to develop a relationship with the Holy Spirit, and He brought me closer to God. It was like I was sitting on a mountaintop. I could see everything below me, and I was able to see the forces that were driving people in the wrong direction.

The Father said, "I gave my Son in sacrifice for these people, yet there isn't much being done to make them change direction. I have marked that direction with the blood of my Son. Therefore, go onto all nations and tell them the good news. For there are not many who want to go and tell others about my great plans for all who believe in my Son Jesus."

That was one of the things that inspired me to get baptized. I wanted to go and tell everyone that there were only two places to go after someone dies. I was fascinated with what Jesus said in John 14 and Mark 9 and 44. I could visualize those two places, and I felt a sense of urgency to announce to the world that something was awaiting us. I had a picture in my mind of a huge line of people walking on a road that ended in a bottomless pit. They were falling down and had no chance to go back and warn the others. I could see the agony and regret of the people going down. For them, there was no return. I wanted to transmit these images to people in the same way I was visualizing them in my mind. I thought of holding up a sign and shouting, "Stop. Don't go there." Anyone on that road was destined to remain in that place of darkness forever. I regret that we can't do anything for those people. I pictured someone desperately trying to rewind the time and be able to make a different decision. A decision that can change a destiny forever, but there is nothing anyone can do to bring themselves back to the world of the living.

I was trying to do everything according to the scriptures because I knew my salvation would be secured. The pastor set the date, but I was nervous. It had to be on a Sunday during the raining season. I would have to be exposed to the people watching the soccer game. The entire village would be watching the game. For tournaments, people from other villages and towns came. My pastor thought it was a great opportunity to witness to the lost. We knew that everyone who gathered there were not good Christians. They were sinners in need of a Savior, and I was going to be a living testimony to all of them, so they could see that age didn't matter when someone wanted to serve the Lord.

In early May, we went down to prepare the baptismal pool. Some of the church elders, my father, and I accompanied the pastor at the front of the group. With a simple *machete in hand*, a shovel, and the wiliness to serve, we created a beautiful blue-green pool that would bury my sins and the sins of the people who were being baptized. We finished around eleven, and the baptisms were scheduled for three.

A great number of people were heading to the game, and a handful of people were heading to celebrate the baptisms. I wanted the day to be over as soon as possible. I knew all my friends would be watching, and that made me nervous. I was the only one of the young people from that village who was crazy enough to go into to that pool. They saw me like an extraterrestrial doing something that didn't make sense. There was no way to make it private or change the date.

To make matters worse, people used to sit along the creek—no more than ten meters uphill from where I was going to be baptized. The few trees on that side were not enough for privacy. As good Christians, we were supposed to shine in the darkness. I was not ready to have all those people watching me being baptized. I was afraid that they would stone me while I was in the pool, and I was not ready to be a martyr. It was an agonizing time for me, and there was no one to rely on for consolation. I felt my heart pounding, but it never crossed my mind to go back on my decision to be baptized. I felt the pressure of my surroundings. I went to a little dark corner to pray and asked the Lord for strength to carry on with what He had commanded me to do. I didn't want anyone to know I was afraid. I didn't tell my parents that I was afraid because I didn't want them to think I was weak in faith. I wanted them to believe I was a genuine Christian, and baptism was one way to prove it to them.

At three o'clock, I was ready to walk down to the creek where I had spent my childhood swimming with my friends and cousins. This time, I was going without them. I was going to do something that didn't make sense to them. It was something I had to do—even though I couldn't fully explain why. It took us no time to get there. There were some of the others who were also being baptized, but they didn't offer me any moral support because they were from another generation. I was going to look around and say goodbye to the world and say goodbye to myself. In a few minutes, I was going to be buried in that pool and come out a new man. As a local boy who knew what was usually going on around that creek, the miracle had already started. Finding the pool in the same condition as we left it was a miracle. With all the people around, it wouldn't take long for them to release the water since it was being retained with stones, branches, and sand. They knew we were going to be interrupting their soccer game since we were going to be having a full service beside it, and it was a miracle they didn't vandalize it. They didn't agree with it, but it was something they feared. That was why they didn't dare touch it before we finished our ceremony.

It was customary for the church to have a service wherever the baptisms took placc. Whether they take place at the beach, at a river, or somewhere else, there would be a full service. The assistant pastor was in charge of preaching, and the pastor was going to baptize us. The preacher was so happy to be the guest speaker since he was the one God used to pull me out of the pew six months prior. That was the ultimate confirmation of his calling from God. As all the candidates for baptism lined up in our white robes, I looked toward the soccer field to see what was going on. I saw a crowd racing toward the creek. It was the one thing I was afraid of. They found our event more fun to watch than the game. From that moment forward, I didn't lift my head again. I focused on the water and waited for my turn to be baptized.

It was amazing how the Holy Spirit brought total control among the crowd as we were being submerged. I am not sure if they stopped the game to watch us.

As I was about to be submerged, my older brother said, "What great courage in that kid." He was the goalkeeper, but he had to come watch me being baptized.

The pastor asked if I had a few words, but I couldn't talk. I thought it was better to leave that part out and carry on with the program.

There was no applause, special signs, or voices from heaven when I came out of the water. I was the same person who had gone in minutes before. There was nothing different in me, but I was sure I had accomplished my goal. In my heart, I felt like I had Jesus's approval. I was in complete harmony to His Word. With my head down, I made my way out from the pool.

My father was waiting with a white sheet to wrap me with at the edge of the pool. He said, "Well done, son." Then he wrapped me with the sheet and patted my shoulder, and I had never felt so much love coming from him. I felt like I was being embraced by Jesus himself.

It was a feeling of acceptance from my father—and my heavenly Father was welcoming me into the kingdom of heaven.

From that point forward, my life as a teenager changed in many ways. The Holy Spirit brought me to a different level, and the things pertaining to this world didn't matter for me anymore. My fears were drowned in that pool, and I had no other desire than to follow Jesus. Even though there were not many people who shared that same dream with me, I was on fire for the Lord. The only teenagers were the pastor's daughter and the pastor's assistant's daughter, but we didn't talk much. I had to rely on the little teaching I could get from each service and time alone with my Bible. It wasn't enough for my spiritual growth, but if I trusted God with all my heart, I knew I would go where Jesus wanted to take me.

I have seen hundreds of baptisms. Some of them were really exciting, and some of them were no more than just a walk to a pool. Perhaps the real sense of it has been lost since many people do not have the devotion that is needed. It was a life-or-death matter, and I couldn't see myself not fulfilling that part of the scripture.

I was constantly being terrorized by my fears and people who had no respect for my beliefs or for me as an individual, but I was able to go through with it. In spite of all I had to go through, God picked that moment for me to witness in front of almost the entire village. God used that moment to let those people know He loved them. I finally understood how much my father loved me, and I got to feel the love of the heavenly Father like I had never felt it before. I felt like God had clothed me with another garment.

From that moment forward, all those who mocked me were ashamed because the love of my heavenly Father had given me a new status. I could see the future through the Word of God in a way that was impossible for a teenager to explain. I wanted to tell everyone about the danger of living without God. Dying without Christ was a total loss. I could see hundreds of people going to hell, and I felt regret that nothing could be done.

I pictured hell and the people who were going there. I felt pain for them because the saving hand of Jesus had been shortened for them. My mission was to do what God had called me to do, and I was going to make a difference in my village. I did not know what was ahead, but I would rely solely in the promise of God. He was going to be with me forever.

CHAPTER 5

A New Preacher in the Village

For I am not ashamed of the gospel of Christ:
for it is the power of God unto salvation to
everyone that believeth. To the Jew first,
and also to the Greek. For therein is the
righteousness of God revealed from faith to
faith: as it is written, the just shall live by faith.

—Romans 1:16

After my baptism, everything changed for me. It was like I had awoken to a new world. The Holy Spirit was showing me the reason why He had chosen me. I realized I had been afraid and ashamed all along. The pressure of my surroundings was enormous, and that was one of the reasons why I couldn't lift my head to look all the people who were looking at me when I was being baptized.

The Word came to me and pointed to the power of the Gospel. The Holy Spirit showed me that I was not alone. I was going to be able to fulfill my call. I felt like I had all the tools to carry on with the mission for what I was being commissioned. I was going to open my mouth, and the Holy Spirit was going to do the rest. I was certain that my encounter with God had been real. That assurance led me to consecrate my life for Jesus. My only comfort and counsel was the Holy Spirit. There was no one else to rely on because everyone was doing their own thing. We did not even have a structure to call a church. We were focused on building the people's church first, and then we would build a church for the community.

The mission was on to save the village, and there was no time to waste. It was going to be possible, and I had been called. God had promised to be with me always. Armed just with my Bible, I was ready to let the locals know it was dangerous to live without Christ. Nothing matters if we live apart from God, but there is hope in Jesus Christ. Without a pulpit or a title, I began to preach to every person I knew or ran into. On my way to work in the fields or on my way to church or on my way to town, I spoke about salvation in Christ Jesus. I felt compelled to speak about Christ in every situation. Whether it was a young or old person, I needed to let them know something was coming. Where would they be when it happened?

I knew there was going to be an opposition because Catholicism was deep-seated in our culture—and to say that there was no other name but the name of Jesus in my community, there was going to be a problem. That forced me to spend more time in the Word of God to prepare to communicate the Gospel of Jesus Christ.

It was amazing to see how some people reacted to the Word—and I was only fifteen. A man stopped to listen to me while I was grazing one of my horses. He had visited the services when we had them at home, but he never had the courage to say yes to Jesus. He leaned against a fence, and I preached to him about where he was going to spend eternity if he didn't receive the gift of salvation. When the Holy Spirit confronted him, he opened his eyes and saw the future without God. I could see the power of the Holy Spirit convincing him. I could tell he was able to see his picture after death, and he was not comfortable with it. He asked what was needed to avoid going there, and how would he be strong enough to say no to the things of this world.

The Holy Spirit continued touching lives in that community, and we had a revival where many people began a new life in Christ. More young people were going to the services, including some of the soccer players. They were listening in church, which would have been impossible in previous years. There were some kids whose parents were totally opposed to the Gospel, but they were in church.

The Word of God was making an impact in my village. I felt that I had to do more in order to bring the Gospel to every corner of that village. Although there was still a great opposition, I wasted no time spreading the Word to all I could get to. Everybody from that place knew who I was, and for some of them, it was better to avoid contact with me since they knew they couldn't argue with me about God or my faith. My mission was to convey the message of Christ Jesus to everybody—young or old— and I had no fear about letting them know Jesus was the only way to salvation. People looked at me like I was from another world, but God used me to minister His Word to those who would never set foot in church, giving them an opportunity they would never get again. In His omniscient way, He knew what was coming next.

The church was gaining momentum. What started as one family became a large group of people who were growing in faith. Although we didn't have a church building yet, we had a great desire to preach the Gospel throughout the region. The pastor had a bigger vision. He wanted to get a sound system, but that was kind of difficult. We were about two hours away from the power lines, and it would require an enormous amount of money to get hydro towers through those mountains. The second option was a generator, but that was also complicated. Besides the cost of the generator, we would be stuck with maintenance. The fuel was also about two hours away. To make things worse, the only way of transportation was horses or carrying it ourselves.

After a meeting, we decided to look for something

more affordable—even if it wasn't a heavy-duty one. They agreed the best solution to the problem was a twelve-volt system operating by a regular car battery. We also had to recharge the battery, and that was going to be possible only by bringing the battery to the closest city. If we wanted a microphone, we had to do whatever was necessary to power it.

The pastor journeyed to one of the big cities in search of his dream. His mission was to come back with the equipment, and he was able to get exactly what he was looking for: a twelve-volt amplifier, two nice speakers, and two microphones. It was a great step forward for the church. We were able to take the message of the Gospel beyond the borders of our village. We used to hang the speakers in a tree—and even people in other villages were able to hear us. For some people that was okay, but others hated us even more.

The house of worship was situated on the mountain, which allowed us to reach more people with the Gospel. We would hear comments that the halleluiahs were too noisy, that they couldn't sleep, and that it was rude of us. We knew it was impossible to please everyone. We wanted to deliver the message of salvation to everyone in the region.

Soon after that, we got together and made plans to bring the Gospel to other villages. God opened doors elsewhere. The good news reached people in the surrounding villages—thanks to the new sound system.

It was incredible how far we could reach. It was like the sound waves were moved supernaturally throughout the region. We were impressed by the long distances we could cover every night we celebrated our services.

Some people learned about Jesus's love and about our church. In some cases, we were invited to preach in people's homes in other villages. We were prepared. All the men from the church were ready to help with the equipment. We had to walk for more than an hour with a big battery on our shoulders. We made a nice wooden box for the battery that was supposed to be easier to handle, but after twenty minutes, it was not much fun. We only had a few flashlights because not everyone could afford one. We were doing the impossible to get to our destination and do what Jesus had commanded us to do. The villagers by then, were more accommodating to the Christians. We felt more secure to be traveling across villages without fearing being hurt. At the beginning, the church had gone through a very difficult time of persecution, and we were enjoying the freedom.

We managed to deliver the message of Jesus Christ throughout our village and reached parts of the neighboring villages. In some cases, we had to go to the extremes to get to those people. Some people lived in remote areas that not even horses could get to. We used the loudspeaker to spread the Gospel through the mountains because we wanted to give people the opportunity to listen the plan of salvation.

Most of the people who lived in the valleys heard the

Gospel as clear as the people who were in the church meetings. We had church services near the top of a volcano, and all the people who lived near the volcano had the opportunity to hear the Word of God. For some of them, it was the first time that they had heard the Gospel and hearing that Jesus loved them. We were going to do whatever was in our power to tell them that someone loved them. His name is Jesus. We didn't care what distances we had to travel. We left in the early afternoon to make it during daylight since it was no fun being trapped in the mountains at night. In the rainy season, the muddy trails were almost impossible to walk on. To make things worse, we had to go through wet grasslands at night with a lantern and a few flashlights. Sometimes we could guide ourselves with the dim light in the distance from those who lived along the way. We were excited because we could see the hand of God at work. We were not laboring in vain. Many people were coming to the Lord, and the Holy Spirit was witnessing with a powerful manifestation that could be felt from far away.

God was raising up another church in a village about ten kilometers away. It seemed like God had that region marked for a purpose. The Gospel was being preached simultaneously, and the people we couldn't reach were being preached to by the other church. It was like an extension of our church—continuing the work we couldn't do.

A man from another jurisdiction started witnessing in other villages. God raised him, and he was delivering the message of salvation like there would be no tomorrow. He came to our meeting and had a deep conviction about Jesus. He delivered a message I hadn't heard before. He was the only believer in his community. He had a call to the ministry, and he wanted to impact his community, which was very far away.

It was impossible for our church group to visit his location. It was important to help him carry the Gospel to those people. I was compromised with the Lord more than ever, and I was seeing the power of God at work with my own eyes. What started with just one man and his wife had grown exponentially. More than three villages had been reached with the Gospel, and people were being saved despite the opposition we had endured.

My faith had gone to a different level. I was no longer afraid of carrying on with the commandment to take the good news to everywhere I went. Convincing people of the need for a Savior was the greatest joy. I saw how the Lord was changing lives. People who were deep into their religion were trying to be different because they had connected with the throne of God.

My village was on the top of the mountain—physically and spiritually. Most of the people were compelled to see what it really meant to be a Christian, and there was a stronger sense of unity. I saw how the Holy Spirit brought submission to a lot of them. I was not afraid of them pulling a *machete* on me, because something was holding them back. It was a miracle to see these people being receptive to the Word of God. Some committed their lives to Christ. Even the man who thought he was the prophet Elijah had an opportunity to hear the Gospel the right way. We were there to help him to find the way. He no longer needed to be intoxicated to believe he was Elijah, but he could become who God wanted him to be and be used for God's glory.

Every time he got drunk, he thought he was Elijah, and as he was bound by the power of Satan, there were many more like him. He had an opportunity to hear the Gospel—without setting foot in the meetings—and he had an opportunity to be set free.

The love of God had been manifested to everyone in my village and the surrounding villages. I couldn't comprehend how God had stirred up the heart of the man who started preaching in the village. Everybody was aware of something inevitable coming in the near future. The messages was to prepare for the final day.

Men, women, and children heard about eternal hope. God had spoken through people like the pastor and me, and we had committed our lives to the cause of the Gospel. I had contributed to the evangelization of my village, and the seed that had been planted in people's hearts would serve its purpose in time.

I preached and explained the Word to an uncle who was three times older than me. He never took me seriously, but when he was faced with death, I believe God gave him a chance to make things right.

CHAPTER 6

Things Begin to Turn Ugly

The thief cometh not, but for to steal, and to kill,
and to destroy: I am come that they might have
life, and that they might have it more abundantly.

—John 10:10

Since the beginning of time, jealousy has been the key
for destruction. For what was to come next, there is no
other explanation other than Satan and his jealousy for
what God had been doing. My place of birth had been
like a paradise to me and to all who had been born there.
The crystal-clear creek had cleansed the sins of many
through the baptism, and it was about to become red.
Those beautiful mountains surrounding my village
were witnesses for so many encounters with God in the
loneliness of the nights. Countless sermons were preached

in the open air. They were about to witness something that wasn't anything like it.

In the spring of 1980, things begin to turn toward the unimaginable. Our village was on the verge of destruction, and we didn't even know it. A report made its way through the village that the government had us on a list of antigovernment people. They called us enemies of the state. At first, we didn't worry about it since such of claim was simply propaganda. Who would believe such a thing?

We kept on doing the work of God as usual, but some people thought we should do something about it. Another rumor was that the government forces were moving in—and that in our village, "even the dogs were antigovernment" and were trained for war. Again, we carried on with our mission. We were moving forward with our church construction plans. We already had the land that one of the members of the church had donated. He let us pick where we wanted to build on his property.

We agreed to build close to my house. We were excited that we were finally going to have a church and would no longer have services under a hut built from just four posts and some hay for the roof. We were collecting the money for construction, and more bad news came along. It was more credible. Some people started making plans to move out of the village.

I consulted with my father, and since he had done nothing wrong, he wasn't going anywhere. He had been born and grew up there. Everything he had was there, and there was no other place he could call home. Nobody imagined him moving away from his beloved village. That place had given him everything he had and had made him who he was.

We continued getting the land ready for the first crop of the year and pretended that nothing was going to happen. We began hearing rumors that the army was moving into the rural areas of the country in pursuit of the "guerrillas." It brought some comfort to us because we knew our village had been a distinct one. Our priority was always to thrive in everything and not get involved in harmful things. It was good if they came. That way, the whole myth of the "guerrilla" thing would be over. If they came, they would see that everybody was occupied with getting ahead in their own affairs.

Soon, we heard there was more to it. It was more like a war. In other towns and villages in the province, government forces had encountered resistance from antigovernment forces. As a result, villages were being hammered by the army by land and by air, leaving behind devastation. That news was not what we wanted to hear, and it was happening not too far from our village. I had seen no war in my life, and I was dismayed by the news. My heart pounded as I tried to find a solution. No one knew what to do next.

A few weeks later, we heard another report. This time, it was much worse. It was like an informant was reporting from the inside, and none of the good and honest people knew who the person was. We never paid attention to the details if anyone accused us of being "guerrillas."

The bad news was that our village was going to be hit next. We were in the eye of the army. Therefore, the army was going to come to our village and kill everyone. If even our dogs were part of the guerrillas, there was no chance to escape or come clean.

Panic began to take over among the villagers. The men started to wrap up blankets and get ready for nightfall. They were going to spend the night in the woods and leave the women and children at home. My father and I didn't want to hide. We had done nothing wrong. Why should we go into hiding? We stayed home, and the rumors were coming and going. It gave us a little bit of time to carry on with our crops.

We didn't know what was going to happen next. We had no other choice but to continue moving forward. Since we had no subsidies to rely on, we had to keep moving. If we didn't, we were going to have another problem. We would be facing starvation. Resiliency was ingrained in us. We were strong, and we were going to make it out of that situation. We didn't know what the whole ordeal was, but we believed we were innocent. It was going to be proven once and for all.

After a few more weeks, everything seemed to be forgotten. We were going ahead with our plans to make our village great. Our vision included our well-being, material things, and the new place of worship. For a moment, it was like we had gone inside the eye of the storm. All seemed calm, and we felt we shouldn't be concerned. If we moved on, our government would see we were improving our village. We believed our government was interested in its people. Instead of destroying the place, they were going to leave us alone. After they saw there were no weapons, we thought they would walk away. We heard that other places in the country were being destroyed. Clashes between the rebels and the army were leaving many people dead. We knew things were not as simple as we had thought. Knowing we were on the blacklist made us even more nervous.

We started seeing signs of war throughout the country, and we heard news on the radio of many places being attacked by the army. It was on a much higher scale. Villages were being bombarded, and masses were being killed. We could see helicopters in the distance. Rural areas were being bombarded, and smoke was rising from those places. Although we heard the bombs going off, there was no way to see exactly what was going on. The news that was being broadcast was about the heroes who were putting their lives on the line by trying to defend themselves and the people from the villages. For them, all the people they were killing were guerrilla fighters, and that was what they were there for. When a villager was killed, it was enough to frame him by putting a gun on him and say that he was a rebel killed in action. The media was being controlled and saying only what they were permitted to say.

After some of the survivors escaped, we learned what was going on. We were facing a mountain we couldn't climb. Our possibilities were next to zero. Trying to move out was never considered. There was nowhere to go. War had broken out all over the country, and the rural areas were affected the most. The cities were being spared for the time being, but fights broke out here and there. The firepower was more benign than in the rural areas.

It was impossible to move the livestock. Maybe people could leave their houses behind, but it wasn't an option for those who owned more than land and houses. Even if we tried to go to another region, we still were going to be monitored by the government for being part of the antigovernment movement. There was nowhere to turn, and we were left only with the possibility of facing the danger. We were not armed or trying to defend ourselves. We were simple people with just the tools to work the land. We had seen no one from the village getting involved in anything antigovernment or any guerrillas coming by or conducting any activities of any kind. Most of us had no idea what was going on with the war that was being brought to the rural areas. We had seen nothing like it in the entire history of the country, and we were about to get into a war that we had not asked for. We were standing on the path of destruction and had no possibility of getting out of the way. We had no idea of the magnitude we were going to be hit with. A large number of people were trying to find a solution. They were trying to save their lives, land, and their precious possessions, and they were trying to save their way of living and culture.

We were being tortured by the rumor of war, and we didn't know when or how it was going to come to us. We were not prepared in any way for it. We used to get up every morning and feel happy to carry on with our activities, tending our cattle and all the rest of the other animals, and we were going to wake up to see the destruction of our loved ones or die. It was torture.

Parents were trying to save their children, but they didn't know how. How were they going to explain to their children that danger was on the way? The people who they had trusted for protection were not able to defend them. Instead, the parents were going to be tied up to a tree and tortured or forced to watch their kids being raped and killed in front of them. It was an agonizing time. The army had no regard for anyone or for any living thing. Where could one hide when they had all the big guns and bombs?

That frightening period didn't make us wait too long. We had no idea we were entering into the gates of Hades, and there was no one we could call for help. No one knew how to make it to the other side. Young and old and women and children were in the same tunnel of annihilation. Everything we had accomplished was going to be gone. We were seeing the present moment like we were going into a sinkhole that we couldn't get out of. Instead, we were going deeper and deeper by the minute. We tried to look to the future, but we had been robbed of it. The old saw their children fatherless if they managed to survive that catastrophic era, and mothers lost their children to both armies. Whether to the left or to the right, there were no guarantees.

In June 1980, I got up as usual to go to work the fields. I was scheduled to go to one in a remote area. There were larger areas that were used for cattle and farming. The area was also connected to a district that wasn't on the blacklist.

I grabbed some tools and checked for hay for my horses. I was just in the middle of the soccer field when I heard the first shot. I thought they were shooting at me since I was the only person walking across the field. I had no choice but to throw myself to the ground and roll to the other side of the field where the shrubs were high enough to take cover.

When I reached the bushes, I got up and ran down a trail that connected to other villages. I ran without knowing if it was an ambush coming from all directions, but my first instinct was to go in that direction to save my life. I didn't run into a single soul along the way. I went deeper into the woods and hid in a place where I was able to see most of the village. My village was going up in flames. I heard the shooting that was taking place in the village and in the village that was next to it. Every shot I heard was being shot straight at the people.

Evil forces broke loose, and innocent people were being murdered without mercy. Who were we supposed to call for help if the ones who were supposed to protect us were murdering us? I wasn't able to hear the screams of the people being murdered. I was hiding and running away from my house. I could see the smoke from both villages. I felt safe in my place of refuge, but I didn't know how safe my parents and siblings were. I remained hidden until I felt it was safe to go back and see if I still had a house and family to go to. There was no way to communicate with my people. I thought I was going to be in that place for a long time.

For hours, I didn't know what to do. What if they did something terrible to my family? What would I do? I thought they had burned my house. Why didn't my father leave before me? He was always the first one to leave for work. Why had he stayed behind this time? All these grim ideas came to mind about what was happening—and there was nothing I could do about it.

Every hour that went by was an eternity. I didn't know what was going on with my family. Was I going to be an orphan? If so, how was I supposed to make it on my own? A thousand thoughts went through my mind. How was I going to cope with this tragedy? Everything was in plain sight for me. I didn't need too much to see that something had changed for me that day.

My stomach stuck to my spine, and my tongue stuck to the roof of my mouth I had no other choice but to wait. I was alone with God in the woods as I waited for a signal to return home. The hours went by, and I was not ready to face reality. As it got later, I started to hear less shooting. The shooting was moving toward the other village, but the smoke was still rising. It was about twelve or so, and something told me not to move yet. *It is not safe to move from here.* I thought I was going to stay there until dusk. If the army didn't want to spend the night there, I could navigate at night if I had to.

Around two o'clock, all shooting stopped. The smoke was dying down, and I started making my way home—if I still had one. It never crossed my mind that the army could be searching for evidence that would support the information they had against my village. All I wanted was to go home and see what had happened.

I began walking cautiously toward my house. It was the longest walk ever. They could be waiting to see who would show up, and I could fall into their trap. From seven in the morning until around three, I didn't see another living soul. Everyone had vanished or gone somewhere, but there was no other option but to see for myself where I was going to go from there. From that point on, my future became uncertain. What if nothing was left of my village? What if they had massacred all the people? I had heard horror stories from other villages. From what I had seen, anything could have been possible.

The soccer field was empty, and I didn't hear a single noise from my house. The view was blocked by some mango trees, and it wasn't clear enough to see what had been done to my family. The pressure was on to go closer to my house, but I didn't see any smoke rising. I thought it could only mean two things. Either the fire had consumed my house and there was nothing left to burn, or they had spared my house and my family. If they were fine, why hadn't they sent someone to look for me?

How could my father and my mother have forgotten all about me? They knew I had just left home when the shooting started. A company of soldiers had come down to the creek, and that was why they couldn't see me when I was going across the field. They started shooting and made their way toward our house. If they had seen me, I wouldn't be telling this story. The silence only made me more anxious. What mother would forget her child in such a circumstance?

I could have been dead in the woods, and no one was looking for me. I had no choice but to walk toward my house to find out what had happened. I was cautious and took a small trail through our property to avoid any danger. Our house was still standing. Even the addition where the girls used to do all the cooking was still standing. I was excited that our house hadn't been burned, and I ran to see everyone and hear what had happened.

Everyone was still in one piece, but they were all in shock. My father was still trying to pull himself together, and my mother and the other children were frightened. Some of the kids who were running around told me about two bodies down by the creek—we got together and ran down to see those two bodies. When we got there, I realized those were the shots that made me throw myself to the ground when I was going across the soccer field that morning. It could have been me. I knew the two men by name, and they had run in the same direction as me. The only difference was they went down the creek, which ran parallel to the trail I had taken.

No one dared to touch them. Most of the people were afraid, and some of the men who had managed to escape were still hiding. The kids were also talking about other people who had been killed and the houses that had been burned. I began to sense the spirit of death in the air, and I ran back to my house to see what was next.

My parents were kind of confused. They had no clue what they were supposed to do, and daylight was running out. The bodies needed to be picked up and carried to the other side of the village. One of the men was from the far corner of the village, which was about forty-five minutes away. Something had to be done, but no one knew what to do. It was a big task for those whose lives had been spared. We didn't know if the soldiers were returning. We were afraid to go out in the open. We had to do something before the corpses began to decompose, or to do something before domestic animals would tear them apart since there were no fences for these animals.

When I got back to the house, my mother and my sisters told me about the ordeal they had to endure. The soldiers lined them up and asked my father if he was part of the antigovernment movement. While he was being interrogated, others were checking the blacklist. They told my father they were going to find his name on the list, and then they were going to kill him. It didn't matter what one said—if the name appeared on the list, there was nothing that anyone could do.

According to my sisters, the first soldier couldn't find my father's name. They read it again because they were sure my father's name was on the list. Others were checking his identification to make sure they had the right man. They held my brother at gunpoint and looked for his name on the list so they could shoot him as well.

My father and brother were the only two men in the house at that moment, and they were the focus of the interrogation and torture. The women and children were pushed away. My uncles who lived at my grandpa's home managed to get away and hide. My grandparents, the women, and the children were left behind. The woods surrounding our home was thick enough to hide, and that was the salvation for those who had time to run before the army got there. My father and brother had no chance to run away, and my father had no fear because he had done nothing wrong. He wouldn't find forgiveness if something had happened to his children and my mom. He would have preferred to die instead of any of us. He knew the atrocities being done by the army, and he wanted to protect his family regardless of the consequences.

The army left my house and continued their assault on the village. They combined forces with another unit to cover the village next to ours. They were killing people and burning their houses without mercy. There were no guerrillas to fight them. It was only frightened, unarmed people who were trying to stay alive.

It was more than chaos. Women and children were crying, and a feeling of death was in the air. Every family had been affected and traumatized. Every family was trying to help since there was no one else to rely on. We had nowhere to go for help.

When I saw my parents, I realized I didn't have it the worst. I didn't see the people, but the devastation they left behind showed who they were. They had no respect for any living thing. They were passionate about destruction and inflicting pain and death on their fellow human being, and they continued terrorizing the two villages for the rest of the day. The families who had lost everything, including family members, were in despair. They needed help burying their dead, but there was not much help since almost everybody had been affected. Families had to bury their own by themselves.

It was getting dark, which made things harder to deal with. We were in a situation we never imagined. Even though all of us in our house were fine, it was a place that none of us wanted to be in. We finally understood the rumors from the villages that had been destroyed before us. Somehow, we thought we were going to be spared. We thought whatever had happened elsewhere was not going to happen in our village. We knew each other, and we knew that no one was involved in any kind of crime.

We took our safety for granted. If the army was looking for armed antigovernment people, they were not going to find anyone fitting those descriptions. We deceived ourselves by trusting the justice system for our protection—we didn't know we had it all wrong trusting them. When these people set foot on our soil, it was like the devil had come against us. There was no place to hide or escape. If we tried to move to another village, we were not welcome because we were being persecuted. These other villagers didn't want to bring destruction to their villages by allowing us to move in. The people from villages that hadn't been affected by war were afraid to open their doors to us. They thought we were involved in something, and they were not going to get mixed up with us. It was our problem, and we were responsible for finding a solution.

Daylight was fading away, and the situation was getting worse by the minute. Cattle and pets were wandering free, and dogs were barking like they sensed more danger on the way. That made the place feel like the soldiers hadn't left. People whose houses were spared didn't want to step out. They thought the soldiers would come back and finish them off.

I was more afraid than when I had run away in the morning. We all felt that our lives were hanging by a thread, and there was nothing we could do to save ourselves. Nobody could sleep that night. Some families had multiples burials, and people had nothing left of their houses. At this point all of us were united, and everyone needed help.

The night passed, and we were glad it was over. There was a better chance of escaping during the day. We weren't sure if they would come back to finish what was left of us. The people who had to bury their dead were taking care of the task themselves, and some thought of running away while they could and leaving whatever they owned behind. Their properties, livestock, pets, and friends could be left behind to save their lives—but that didn't guarantee they were going to make it since their names had been linked to criminal activities. Even when it wasn't true, they were still suspect so they had to do whatever it took to stay alive.

Some children and elderly people were greatly affected. With nowhere to go, we had to endure hardship where we were. Our closest neighbors were left homeless, and their sons were murdered. That was one of the most heartbreaking cases in our community. The fathers of the young men were members of our church. They were faithful to the Lord, yet they were counted with the evil ones. We used to have church services in their homes, and every time there was a church activity, they were the first ones to sign up. Now they were facing the unthinkable and had nowhere to go.

Listing each tragedy would be an enormous task. Satan had traced our path where we used to preach the Gospel, and that path was used to carry out the massacre against the same people we were ministering the Gospel. We didn't realize the sense of urgency when we were preaching a few months earlier. The message was delivered literally: "Run for your life."

We had fought against the forces of evil to bring the Gospel to our village without knowing that the time was over for some of them. We put our efforts into evangelizing in every corner of the village, and spread the message of the Gospel. Even when tragedy caught us by surprise, God knew what was coming. He sent the message of salvation throughout the region.

The next day, the two bodies near my house were picked up by relatives who had managed to escape. They cautiously came out from where they were hiding and gathered some men to help carry the bodies back to where their houses used to be. Everyone was scared because there was a rumor that the army was coming back.

One of the men lived about six blocks away from my house, and the other man lived near the other village that had been attacked. He was trying to escape, and he was letting everyone know what was happening behind him so they could run away if they wanted to save their own lives. He ran into the other man, and they decided to go down by the creek. The timing couldn't have been worse. They reached the end of the line. If they had gone a few minutes earlier, their lives would have been spared.

A company of soldiers was setting up an ambush and were coming down toward my house. The two men did not know what they were running into. Running just a few steps down the creek would have saved their lives. I had gone past that spot just minutes before the men. It made me wonder if the men had taken my place and died instead of me. I believe the shots that I heard on the soccer field were the shots that killed the two men. I had been guided to a different path, and it saved my life. When I got up from the ground, it felt like someone was pushing me to run faster than ever before. I never felt alone while I was running. Even when I heard bullets flying overhead, I had a sense of protection. I didn't know I was running in the right direction, but something told me to keep running to safety.

On the second day, all the house fires had been extinguished. There was no fire department to call or any equipment to use. People were confused about what was coming next, especially those who had lost everything and their loved ones. Some of them had to grab whatever they had left and become refugees. We were abandoned by everyone. There was not a single reporter who had the courage to go and report what was going on in our village.

We did not even make it on to the national news or international news. All the reporters were either too afraid or didn't care about the civilians who were being massacred. They could have made a difference by telling the world what was happening to us. We were left in a hole where no one knew about us or what was happening to us.

Physically weak and emotionally wounded, some people tried to get out of there. There was no help of any kind available to us. Death had been wandering around the two villages, and anyone who was still standing had a big dilemma: look for another place to live or try to rebuild. Some chose to move away and left their livelihoods behind. Those of us who decided to stay had a new challenge ahead. The whole place had been defiled with burial sites all over, and there was a deep sadness for those who had lost their lives. It didn't matter who those people were. What really mattered was that we were a community—and that community had been split in many pieces.

Everybody knew the people who had been murdered, and they were humble people who had nothing to do with whatever we had been accused of. We didn't know how to deal with that act of violence against humanity. Crimes were never reported or sent to a court for justice. We were supposed to keep them quiet to preserve our lives, and no one dared report the crimes to any authority or the Red Cross and other entities that were there to protect the innocent and supposedly help the victims of war. Nobody took the time to check on us. It was a victory for the government. They had put an end to another village that they knew had nothing to do with what they called an *insurrection*. The names of those who were murdered that day were not important to anyone except their families. For the murderers, their crimes went unpunished—and there was no justice because they were the law.

CHAPTER 7

The People Who Were Murdered

It is unfortunate that we live in a society whose principles are based upon, fame, money, and pleasure—and not the things that matter most. A neighbor could be dying, and it won't matter because we don't feel his or her pain. If we were only to follow the principle of loving one another, the whole world wouldn't be in a state of collapse and decay.

Once certain things make it into our brains, it's impossible to get rid of them: the first day of school, the day we saw the person we fell in love with, or the day we got married. We can go back twenty, fifty, or eighty years, and those memories remain as fresh as the day they happened. We don't have the power to eliminate the bad or ugly that happens. Those dark memories will stick with the good ones—whether we like them or not—and for some people, the bad memories prevail over the good ones. Others never have the chance to run into a good experience and say, "This experience has marked my destiny forever because there hasn't been anything as awesome as this."

There are memories stored in my mind that won't go away no matter what I do or where I go. These memories will not go away because I can't tolerate seeing the innocent or powerless being bullied, taken advantage of, or getting killed.

I am about to describe something that has kept me wondering for many years why no one from the international community did anything about it. Why were all these crimes committed against the innocent in my community. As frightening as it was then, it is still now—that the victims and survivors still have to see and hear about the monsters who had no remorse about killing another human being. They are still running loose in many parts of the Americas. In other countries, they were granted political asylum instead of being put on trial as criminals of war. It is repulsive and illegal to leave them unpunished. Some victims are haunted by the fact that they are still in danger, and they have to stay quiet. There is nothing they can do because the law is failing to protect them once again.

There were many people who were murdered in my village and in the village next to mine, but we were shocked by the way four of my neighbors were murdered. It is not because I only feel sympathy for them and not for the rest of those who suffered the same fate. It is more about the killers who had no remorse about killing their own people. How can a human being delight in performing such a crime and have no conscience about what he is doing? That is wrong and evil. It is nothing more than demonic people who delighted in doing just that. The role of the army is to serve and protect the citizens of its country. Countries have armies so people can feel safe and protected—and not feel nauseous just from seeing them. When they behave worse than barbarians—killing everyone and destroying everything in their path—they have terrorized their own people.

It seemed that these diabolical soldiers came out from the abyss and had no regard for any living thing or human life. When they were unleashed to the countryside, it was like opening the gates of Hades. There was no place to hide. Reporters, media, and the international community were not going to sacrifice themselves by going to all the villages to see what the great heroes were doing to defenseless villagers.

The army was commanded to inflict as much pain and destruction on the people, and there was no one to denounce their crimes. Was this possible due to the lack of education in a third world country? What can someone expect after arming a bunch of idiots and teaching them how to pull the trigger and shoot anything that moves? That wasn't the case with our army. Our army had been trained by one of the best academies of the world: the Americas.

The *Batallón Atlácatl* was responsible for most of the worst massacre during the war—according to, *La Masacre del Mozote en* El Salvador, this battalion apparently was divided by nine companies that were the elites of the whole army. They had been trained at the *Escuela de las Americas* that that the United States operated between 1946 and 1984 in Panama.[1] American involvement only made it worse.[2]

We can't say the army behaved idiotically against civilians because they were not well trained for the war. It was the opposite. They were totally transformed into wild beasts with the only objective of killing and destroying. They had been granted a license to do just that. Their philosophy was to inflict pain on the enemy, use whatever would make them suffer, capture their loved ones, torture them, rape their women and daughters, burn their houses, and kill them. Age and creed didn't matter. It was their way of saying, "We are your worst nightmare, and here we come!"

They were right though, we all saw them as monsters risen from Hades. When I saw those people at checkpoints,

---

[1] numerof.org/fotografia-relato-archivo-la-guerra-civil-salvador/
[2] https://elpais.com. Jan 20, 1981—*La entrada en El Salvador de una gran cantidad de armas procedentes ... ha sido la razón que ha movido a Estados Unidos a reanudar la ayuda militar ... desde el martes, deben darse cuatro condiciones para que una guerra.*

my heart felt like it was going to come out of my chest. Most civilians did not trust or feel protected when we were running into those people. We didn't know if we would make it or be executed along the road. We didn't need a criminal record to be pulled aside and murdered. It was heartbreaking to see them pull someone out of a bus or car at the checkpoints. We knew the person was not going to make it. They were going to end up dead along the road or in a mass grave.

That was our army! It should have protected and served the citizens. Instead, they were bringing desolation and terror to every village. They went where they felt free to exercise their training. As cruel as it sounds, they wouldn't hesitate to use a child or villager as targets for target practice. Those coldblooded killers had no trouble going to sleep after their gruesome crimes. They were brainwashed. If they had to torture their own mothers, they would have. That was the misfortune that two of my neighbors ran into.

Joe and Phil were cousins, and they were in their early twenties. They lived near my house, and they were very bright. One of them used to entertain the kids on the way to school. He and his brothers could make music from anything. Although they didn't have much, it didn't stop them from finding ways to make life easier. My friend and I went to his house and saw a full orchestra made from combining household items and regular instruments. We decided to put them to a test, and before we knew it, we were listening to music that sounded like it was coming from the radio. The bass was one of the coolest instruments of all. He had managed to make the bass from a large tin pot and a tin tube. It was customized to the right pitch. There were no strings on that bass, but it sounded like a real acoustic bass. When he wasn't working the fields, he would be playing music with his brothers. He never got mixed up in any antigovernment protests or other illegal activities that would cost him his life.

His cousin Phil was working his way up toward become a professional photographer. He was serving the community and had a bright future. In the seventies, he was shooting in color and using a large-format camera. He was going in the right direction. He took my first photograph, and he was getting better at his profession. He was an asset to our community. Everyone knew who he was, and he took photos for all types of identification cards. We were not close friends because he was a little older, but he was a bright young man with great potential and a great future.

Unfortunately, the cousins were not able to fulfill their dreams. They didn't deserve such a tragedy. They were serving our community in whatever ways they could. They were not in the wrong place at the wrong time. They were where they were supposed to be. They didn't have to run away and hide. They belonged right where they were—in their home village. They thought they were safe and did not think they would die at an early age.

There was no cause to be on the run since everyone lived harmoniously. Everything that was needed was there. Everyone was happy doing his or her own thing.

When the army invaded our village for the first time, the cousins were captured. For some reason, they were together that morning. Perhaps they were on their way to the fields. Whenever they were not exercising their profession, they were working in the fields or tending their cattle. With nothing to fear, they began to identify themselves.

The army wasn't interested in arresting them or figuring out who they were. They were apprehended on the main road and were at the mercy of the monsters—two defenseless men against a military company armed with heavy weaponry. They had no idea why they were captured. They were law-abiding citizens. The army had surrounded the area. They were like two grasshoppers among thousands of ants. No matter where they jumped, they were going to be devoured.

The soldiers began torturing them in plain sight. It was no problem for the soldiers to kill someone, and they enjoyed killing them bit by bit. They began doing unimaginable things. People were able to hear the screams and pleas for mercy. That makes the case of Joe and Phil hard to think about. People couldn't do anything to help them. It's possible the parents were listening their children being torture and murdered, but they couldn't run to help them. Powerless to do anything to save their love ones, the parents had to endure the pain that was being inflicted on their sons while they were being put to death. For the soldiers, it was a sport to make a human being suffer and eventually killing him or her. They carried on with this atrocious crime until Joe and Phil's voices went silent.

It is unclear how long they were able to endure the torture, but witnesses were able to see the scene. They were set loose to create more excitement. The soldiers found pleasure in seeing a human being jumping to alleviate the pain. The executioners and the rest of the soldiers were enjoying the gruesome scene. It couldn't go on for long. The men could only resist so much before their hearts stopped. When they were no longer alive, they were left in the middle of the road so everyone could see what had happened to them. The people of the east side of the village had to pass by when coming to town, and as well cars were able to make it through that stretch of road. They did these acts to terrorize the village. After they left, everybody was able to see this horrendous crime—including kids.

Without a motive or confrontation of any kind, they were committing heinous crimes against humble people who couldn't defend themselves. The people they were supposed to be after were not there, but that didn't stop them from having their way with the ones who couldn't defend themselves. The "insurgents," as the army called them, were able to put up a fight—and not be killed so easily, but it was easier for the bloodthirsty murderers to line up a bunch of women and children, kill them in cold blood, and file a report for the media they controlled. Then claim that they had found resistance to their operation and were able to kill so many insurgents and seize their weapons. The tactic worked for the government for many years because no reporters cared enough to go report the truth about what was really happening in the remote areas of the country. For the nationals, it was understandable up to a point, but the foreign media was satisfied by the reports that were coming from the military. They were being held up as heroes instead of criminals.

That was the end for Joe and Phil. The cousins woke up that morning and thought it was going to be a normal day. They wouldn't guess that it would be their last one. The pain the parents went through is unimaginable.

The next case about my two other neighbors is quite the same. What is more repulsive is that these soldiers were committed to hurt people in any possible way—leaving the ones they couldn't hurt physically, unable to forget the horror caused to their loved ones. Who in this world would be able to forget the screams of their own child when he or she is being tortured and murdered without mercy? The parents had no choice but to live with the tragedy.

Two other neighbors suffered the same fate. When I got home after the army left that day, some of the little kids told me two more people had been killed. They said, "And you should see the way the soldiers killed them."

I asked who they were talking about, and they were talking about Jake and his uncle James. Their parents' houses were on the same property, and they had everything in common. Our church had been hit too. The parents of these two young men were members of our church, and Jake and James used to go to our church as well. They were supporters of our church and were there when we had services in one of the parents' homes. Whenever there was a need for volunteers for any church activity, they were ready to help. They were part of our church although they didn't attend regularly. Jake had been raised in church, and James had been brought to church as a teen. They had a good understanding of the Word of God. They were not mixed up in any criminal activities.

Jake and I went to the same school, and we had similar horses. The only difference between our horses was the color. The two horses didn't like each other at all, but we were good friends. We liked to race them, but we were not supposed to. It was dangerous to ride the two stallions close to each other since they were always in competition. They were not supposed to be together for even a minute. Sometimes they broke loose and looked for each other to have a fight, and when that happened, our parents had to pull them apart. That wasn't child's play, but we lived for those moments. Danger was our game. Unfortunately,

Jake's life ended at a young age because of a group of people with no regard for life. The parents had a shop where they manufactured all kinds of farming tools. Since farming was the number one thing for all of us, they were always busy. They were important people in our community. People from other communities used to bring their products to the market on weekends, and they were able to supply other communities with their products. They were very busy people who had no time to be mixed up in anything that would hurt anyone. Their passion was to serve our community. The parents never expected to go through such a trial in life. Losing all material things wouldn't have been as devastating as losing their children in a senseless act that no one could make sense of.

The army's plan was to come all at once and surprise everyone. A huge number of soldiers almost covered both villages at once. They managed to surprise a lot of people. The parents of the two men left when they heard the rumors that the army was destroying everything in its path. They left with the rest of the family, leaving James and Jake to take care the livestock.

When the forces of evil broke loose, James and Jake never had a chance to run. They hid in one of their houses. It didn't take long for the army to capture them and set their houses on fire with them inside. The soldiers—apparently elite forces—had captured two insurgents and were going to have fun with them. They killed two humble villagers, and one of them was just a teenager. I can't imagine how the soldiers could enjoy human suffering. What kind of human being sets someone on fire and enjoys watching them burn? How can a human being close his ears to someone who is begging for mercy from inside a raging flame and not be moved? Only a diabolic person would do such a thing and still go sleep without trouble.

That was the fate for my two neighbors whose lives were terminated without explanation. Nobody could stand up for them and give them a chance in life. Their screams for help weren't heard because those who were supposed to protect the innocent were their executioners. Worst of all, they were counted as rebels and enemies of the state.

There was no voice for the innocent. Only the voices of those wearing the uniform of the state were to be heard. The uniform had been tainted with the innocents' blood, and they were still being held up as heroes who were fighting and putting their lives on the line for the people. That was the message being sent throughout the country and the world. Support from the exterior was coming in to help the government combat the insurgents who were responsible for destabilizing the country's economy according reports. At the same time, the blame was put on the insurgents for many of the deaths.

The crimes were always committed to cause pain for the families of the victims. Deep wounds could never be healed and would never be forgotten. Many of the victims' relatives went to their graves wondering why they were selected to go through such horrors. They couldn't forget the cries of their loved one asking their killers to spare their lives.

Those who are still around feel like they are reliving those moments. It is something that was engraved in their minds forever. There hasn't been a sense of closure for them. Time hasn't erased the deep wounds, and it never will. The community will never be the same. It lost great people who were making it and holding it together. Although the church lost some people, it understood the purpose and calling to minister in that community. We understood that we had to quickly deliver the message of salvation throughout the region, but we didn't know why.

That tragic story will always be present in my mind. How could I forget the people who lived close by, especially those who were part of my childhood? Two young men had been there ever since I could remember, and in a moment, their lives were taken. In one moment, they were living their lives to the fullest, and in the next, they were gone. It was not an accident. They were tortured. The cries of those two human beings still resonate among those who knew them. The parents had to collect whatever was left and flee. There was no safe place to go. It was like we were condemned. Everywhere we went, we were watched. We were living on the brink of persecution.

With so many people gone, the village was not the

same. We tried to make it work, and we began to carry on with whatever we had been doing. Some of us had all our crops planted and needed to wait until harvest time. We hoped that whatever had happened was going to be over. We thought that chapter was closed for our village. We were trying to start over, but a lot of the people who had been part of our great community were no longer with us.

In those somber days, we had to figure out how to move on. Although we were strong people with powerful attitudes, it seemed like our spirits had been broken. That cannot be repaired overnight, and none of us could imagine there was more to come. What we had seen was just a prelude for what was yet to come.

Since the army didn't find any resistance, they should have had no reason to go back to our village. We continued with the church. It was stronger than ever, and we helped the community in every way we could. Many people developed a sense of unity toward one another, and there was still no outside help of any kind. We were all we had, and as a community, we had to make thing work.

The years have gone by, but the memories of what happened linger in my mind. The atrocities that were committed, especially to those four neighbors, will be present in my mind forever. It is more repulsive that the names of the victims did not even make it on to the list of civilians who died during the war. They had no recognition, and the murderers were unpunished.

For the families who lost someone, there is nothing

else to do but relive the moments when their loved ones were taken away in the most violent way possible. Those four young lives were ended by evil people, and they didn't stand a chance. They will only live in the memories of those who loved and knew them well.

CHAPTER 8

July 4, 1980

The secret things belong unto the Lord our
God: but those things which are revealed
belong unto us and to our children for ever,
that we may do all the words of this law.

—Deuteronomy 29:29

Why did God let it happen? If He's the almighty God,
why didn't He do anything? Well, there are some things
that we don't need to understand when we trust God.
We don't need to know the reasons why things happened
the way they happened. That would be trying to put
the Creator on our level. We don't have the capacity to
understand the mind of the almighty God. I am not trying
to defend God. He doesn't need a human to defend Him
before those who are always looking for an excuse to blame

Him for whatever happens or for whatever goes wrong in this world. My experience with God goes beyond what my words can explain, but there are things I cannot explain—things like what happened on July 4, 1980. I have been walking with God for the past forty years, and I still can't understand all of God's purposes.

July 4, 1980, was the ultimate test in my life. If not for divine intervention, I wouldn't be telling this story. I have lived through hard times since an early age, but it was nothing like what I had to live through on July 4, 1980, at six o'clock. That moment marked my life with a deep wound. Although time has passed, in my mind, it's still playing like it happened yesterday. Every time I tell my story, it feels like I am going back in time. I find myself going back to the evening when my world came crashing down. I imagine I am standing alone in an empty field—and that I am surrounded by wild beasts that are ready to devour me—but a figure appears and stands beside me, giving me comfort and trust.

About a month after the army went to our village, our worst fears were confirmed. New rumors were circulating that the army was coming, and they were going to wipe us out. Based on our previous experience, we knew the rumors were not necessarily untrue. There were some truth within all of them. Everybody was on alert and ready to hide in the mountains.

We heard they were going to come at night. Some of the men were going to the woods at night, leaving just the women and children at home. My father decided to go into hiding and took me with him. We were not expecting them again since they hadn't found anything that would implicate our village in any antigovernment matters.

We returned to our normal activities and tried to forget what had happened during their first visit. We didn't want to take any chances, and we thought it was better to be prepared. We went deep into the woods for two nights. My father was not much of talker, but during those nights, he tried his best to show me how much he cared for me and the rest of his family.

We slept on very rough terrain in two different locations. We were trying to stay in the most secluded areas, and we knew that no one could be found in those woods, especially at night. My father wasn't happy about leaving behind the rest of his family. "They might be torture by the soldiers if they come" he said. The first thing they were going to ask was where all the men were.

We were hiding in the woods without any way to communicate with the rest of the family. Without knowing what had happened during the night, we would make our way home at sunrise. We made sure we were not running into an ambush. Unfortunately, it didn't take long after the rumors started for the worst nightmare to happen.

My father decided to assist church that Friday instead of going into hiding. He left me in charge of feeding the cattle, and my horse that was tied up beside our house. He took off a few minutes before six since he had to walk about twenty minutes to get to church. It was a beautiful evening with a nice sunset. There was no sign of rain, which was perfect for walking the trails at night.

A few minutes after he left, we heard a big bang in the opposite direction. We couldn't make out what it was, because it was the first time we had heard anything louder than a gunshot. The only thing we knew was that it had come from a place on a hill that was a crossroads for getting down to the valley where we lived, and the other roads led to three more villages.

My mother and the rest of us began to worry because we didn't know if we were supposed to run away or what we had just heard. In that moment of desperation, my father showed up. He knew what was happening right away. He told us a bomb had gone off. "They are here," he said. He went to where we had the cattle, opened the gate, and set them lose. He untied my horse and let it go free. "You are free now." He said to my horse.

My mother tried to reason with him. She didn't want to lose us. "We are women, and I don't think they will do anything to us."

My father refused to go into hiding. He knew what would happen to his daughters and his wife. Since he had done nothing wrong, he didn't think he had to be on the run.

I began to get nervous. I hadn't seen those people up close, and I didn't know what was going to happen. I thought it could be my last day, and I was not sure if

I wanted to be with the Lord at that point in my life. I didn't want to die that young, and if I didn't run away, I was sure I was going to die. A five-foot sixteen-year-old would never stand a chance.

I considered myself a dead man even before the armies got there. My heart began pounding in my chest. Three of my sisters and their kids were running back and forth as I sat on a chair by the front door.

My mother decided to go behind the counter to count the money for whatever we had sold that day. We were doing well with the store since we supplied all the basic groceries to the village. Even people who lived at the border of the other two villages used to shop at our store. My mother hid the money.

My father was pacing back and forth behind the kitchen, and I knew something bad was coming. Within a few minutes, we heard the first gunshots. They were using a high-caliber weapons. Thinking it was going to be my last day, I ran inside to get my Bible. With my Bible open to Romans 13, I began praying that our lives would be spared.

Not long after that, the shooting got louder. It was coming from all directions. The army took over the whole village and the other village they had taken the first time. Within minutes, the shooting had gone mad. They thought the rebels had exploded the bomb to signal the rebels in hiding that the army was coming so they could get ready to fight. The army thought they were under attack and began shooting left and right. They went straight to the people who had nothing to do with being part of the insurgent movement.

We never knew who the so-called rebels or insurgents were, where were they hiding, or how they got there. By detonating a bomb before the arrival of the army and running away, they were putting our lives at risk. That was enough for the army to think we all were part of that movement, and they started shooting everyone without mercy.

The rebels had planned out their escape, and they didn't care about the people who they were putting in harm's way. It didn't take long for the army to take the whole place and start killing everyone they found.

In the valley, it got dark quickly, and that seemed to put pressure on the army to finish the job quicker. There was no time to question anyone. They just lined up everyone they found and shot them.

I was sitting in the chair, reading my Bible, and praying. The shooting was coming closer—and so was the smoke from the houses they had set on fire. The houses that were left standing from the first time were now burning. I was waiting for them to come. I was glued to that chair and had no idea what to do.

When I began to smell the smoke, I ran inside of the house where the merchandise was, knelt on the floor, and leaned against the cashing-out desk. We had two containers of kerosene, about fifty liters in total, that we used to supply the locals for their lighting.

I felt someone tap my shoulder. I totally went into the presence of God interceding for our lives. I was completely abandoned in the arms of Jesus, telling Him to save us from the hands of those who were seeking our destruction. To my surprise, when I opened my eyes, I was face-to-face with one of the most infamous murders.

The government had organized a death squad that operated throughout the country at night. While people were sleeping, they would murder them in cold blood and leave the corpses in the streets for the ambulances to pick up in the morning.

The man was standing beside me— perhaps waiting for me to finish my prayer. He was wearing the army uniform and had a rifle. He asked me to get up and asked me for my name. He never aimed his rifle at me. He just told me that I had to get out because he was going to set the house on fire.

As I was going out to the front corridor, he went behind the desk. He acted like it was a job that had been assigned to him. I never saw him interacting with my sisters or my mom. I thought they probably wouldn't kill all of us, but I didn't know about the two men with high-powered rifles in the front corridor. They had my father on the floor in execution style. I came out of the house with my mom and some of the women who were trying to save whatever they could before he set the houses on fire.

I felt the power of God coming on to me. It took over all my emotions and gave me a sense of control. Everybody was crying, and they still had my father on the ground.

My father said, "If you want to see my documents, I have them here."

I heard no response from the two men.

Our kitchen house was going up in flames, and we were waiting for the other house to catch fire. Since the men were in a hurry, they didn't try hard enough to set both houses on fire. They asked my father to get up because the flames were shooting high up into the air, and they had to go between the two houses to get to the creek.

My father got up, and they grabbed him by the back of his head. They pushed him toward the creek as one of the houses was completely engulfed in flames. When he passed the gate, he turned toward us and said his final words, but I wasn't able to hear them because of the distance.

My little nephew was following closely and heard them.

My father never cared about himself. He always was looking for our well-being. He said, "My children will be homeless." He knew they were taking him to be executed and would never see us again.

There was nothing we could do to save the kitchen house where we had multiple products—including our grain. There was no fire department or water hoses we could use. The creek was close, but even if we tried to fetch any water, there wouldn't be enough time to put out the fire. The attic of the kitchen house was used to store all the product derived from the sugarcane. Which that made it more flammable. That product was like the brown sugar used to sweeten coffee and for doing all kinds of baking. There was no way we could put out the inferno.

My mother went inside to grab the money and some of the rice and beans. She told us to grab what we could—or we would die of starvation.

I wasn't thinking about the future, and my sisters were in shock.

Confused by the scene—seeing the men taking my father, watching our houses going up in flames, and left with only the clothes we were wearing—we didn't know what to make of it. My sisters and my mom were crying and waiting for the houses to be consumed by the fire.

In that moment of desperation, we heard a loud gunshot from the direction where they had taken my father.

One of my sisters screamed, "They killed him."

All the women were crying, having panic attacks, and fainting. I tried to cry, but I couldn't. I began praying for them. I was in another dimension. I was aware of what was going on, but I couldn't relate to the pain and sorrow we were experiencing. It was like something supernatural had taken over me. In my body, I was present, but in my mind, I was with the Lord. Jesus was directing me.

One of the sisters fainted hitting her head hard on the

floor, and I thought she was not going to make it. After I prayed for her, she got up like nothing had happened. I felt like I had to console the rest of my sisters. There was no doubt that my father was dead, but we couldn't look for him until the men were gone.

We were hopeless and couldn't do anything to save ourselves or save my father from the hands of those wicked people. We only had farming tools, and they had high-powered weapons, but the hand of God hadn't been shortened toward His people.

As the fire was about to engulf the storehouse, God heard our cry and sent a rushing wind that blew the flames to the opposite side of the house. That wind was the beginning of what was coming next. Minutes before, I had lifted my head to the skies and asked God to help us. The skies were completely clear, but on the horizon, I saw an orange line. I knew there was no rain in the forecast. The radio people had no way to predict the weather in those areas, and we never paid attention to them. Our way was more accurate. A minute after the gust of wind, we heard a loud bang. It was not from their machine guns. It was coming from above. Help had arrived.

A big storm formed and put out the fire before it went to the next house. The gust of wind kept the flames away from the other house until the rain came down. The rain was better than any fire department at putting out that fire. The thunder was louder than we had ever heard in the village. It only makes sense that it had been created to aid the hopeless. That supernatural rain came from nothing. It was like expecting thunder and rain in the middle of January in New York City when it is twenty below zero.

That impossible rain served a purpose. In the scriptures, thunder represents judgment, and it is possible that the heart of God was filled with grief for what was happening to His children. My father was being sacrificed, and other saints were suffering the same fate.

Nobody wanted to be in the village at night. They were afraid, and they had to get out of the village as soon as possible. They didn't want to take too long carrying out their monstrous crimes. I saw the wrath of God chasing those people out. Even the unbelievers were able to see how fast they were trying to get away from that place. It seemed like someone was finally standing up to them with a greater power.

After they murdered my father, the rain started to get heavier. They had to go up the creek to find their way out. They were shooting, and that's how we knew where they were going. We could see the thunder driving them out of the village. It was like bombers in the skies were shooting at them. The flashes of lightning marked their locations, and the thunder was heard within a minute.

Their gunpower was taken over by the thunder, and we could hear them like firecrackers. The rain and thunder didn't stop until they were all the way up to the mountain, which was where the rebels had set off the bomb. They had to go down that same path since it was the only way to get to town.

After the rain stopped, we couldn't hear any more shooting. We knew they were all over the village, but we never knew all the damage they had done to other people. We only knew they were burning the houses they had left the first time. We didn't have time to think about what was happening to everybody else when we were being tormented ourselves.

Two hours later, the night had come to a standstill. We thought it was time to look for my father. We were all shaking and wanted to find his body before an animal got to him—when we heard a woman crying coming out from my grandparents' home.

Our grandparents lived about five hundred meters from us, but we were not able to see what had happened. Before coming to our house, they had killed my two uncles.

We told her about my father, and she was inconsolable. She thought she had seen enough. We went down to the creek and saw his body under a mango tree. It was hard for my sisters not to cry. As much as I wanted to cry, I couldn't. I removed his hat and saw that half of his skull and his brains were stuck to it.

Weak and broken, my sisters and I carried his body to the store house that had been spared by the fire. Mom had his bed ready, but she hadn't seen his wound yet. I was afraid she would have a heart attack. To make things worse, we had left behind his hat with the rest of his skull. When I saw what was in it, I swung it to the side—and it got stuck in some trees. We didn't spent time looking for it. We thought it was going to be easier to find it in the morning.

While mom was preparing the body, I went over my grandparents to see the other two bodies. My grandparents were in their seventies, and it was heartbreaking to see them crying for the loss of their two sons. I had to find a way to break the news to my grandma.

My grandpa was trying to support my grandma, but he was in bad shape. We thought about telling him the news first. They had to see him for the last time. We brought them over to see their son who had no chance to say goodbye to them. At least the other two were taken in front of them. My grandma even offered the killers money to let her sons live, but they were obsessed with killing. They pushed her away, took them down to a ditch, and shot them in front of everybody. There is no good way to see one's children being killed. It hurts to see your loved ones going out of this world, especially in that way. No one deserves to go through something like that.

We tried to comfort one another by going back and forth between the two funerals all night. We thought the men could come back to finish us off so there wouldn't be any witnesses to their crimes. We thought about the rest of the people of the village. We were overseeing our dead, but no one came to check on us. That wasn't a good thing. We had to figure out how we were going to bury our dead, and we were not prepared. There was not enough manpower to begin with, and where were we going to find three caskets? Even if we did, how were we going to carry them to the cemetery? The cemetery was about one hour away, and we had to walk up a mountain. For normal burials, it took about a dozen men.

I started to feel comfort when I saw the light of the day. It was like all the darkness was an extra weight on me. It didn't take long before we heard what had happened to the rest of the villagers. We heard about all the people who had been murdered in the village next to ours. A large army had invaded the two villages simultaneously. That probably crossed my father's mind when he was going to the church service and heard the bomb. He returned home because he didn't want to leave us alone with those wicked people. He told my mom they were capable of killing all of us if they didn't find the man of the house. He was going to wait for them because he didn't want anything to happen to us.

When the pastor came down to check on us in the morning, he told us what the congregation had gone through. The unimaginable had happened while the others were at our house. He was still alive because of divine intervention. Everyone at church was lined up to be shot. Something happened, and they couldn't pull the trigger. The group of twenty or more were ready to die and had no fear. Church was about to start when they stormed in and questioned all of them about the meeting. When they didn't get the answers they wanted, they decided to kill all of them on the spot. Everybody knew that their time to die had come, and they got ready to meet their Creator. With no regrets for making the decision of coming to church that day, they stood on that line and waited for them to pull the trigger. They began to worship and were ready to face death. No one knows what the soldiers saw when they were about to shoot, but they saw something, put down their weapons, and left.

That night, no one could go home. Some of them had no homes to go to. The soldiers had set all the houses on fire, including some of those belonging to the Christians from church. Fortunately, it was a happy ending for those in that group—with the exception of the assistant pastor. He had been singled out to receive the most horrific news about his daughter Liuna. The troubling news made me sick, and I trembled when I heard what had happened to Liuna. She made me feel welcome in the church every time. We were about the same age, and I could see how much she loved the Lord. She was always trying to do what was right. She helped her mother with the other small children. When we went on mission trips to other villages, she was one of the first to say yes to the cause. Her dreams, desires, and life were taken away in a brutal unexpected way.

She was going to church with her mom when the ordeal began. The services were being held at the pastor's house, and he lived on the upper part of the mountain. It took fifteen to twenty minutes to get there. They walked past a group of soldiers. The mother never thought anything bad would happen to them. What kind of danger could two women on a solitary road be? The army should have been after armed men who could at least defend themselves. When they saw the pretty young girl, they yanked her away from her mother. The mother pleaded with them to leave her daughter alone. They molested her right in front of her mother because rape and murder were what they had been trained to do. It wouldn't be fun for them to spare the young girl, and it would bring more pleasure for them to make the mother watch them rape her. She was like a young gazelle among a bunch of hungry lions. She had no chance to escape unharmed.

They were screaming and pleading for mercy, but no one was available to help them. Even her mother had to abandon her because she had her other baby to save. Hopeless and alone—she was abandoned by everybody and she knew there was no one coming to her rescue. Surrounded by evildoers, her strength began to depart. She couldn't scream anymore. Her cries faded away, and she began to give up. Her pain was even worse when her mother left regardless her pleading not to leave her alone. The only thing for her to do was open her eyes for the last time and say goodbye to her beloved village, since it was the only thing that accompanied her to the end.

The soldiers didn't stop having their way with her until

there was no life left in her. After she expired, they place her body in front of her house and set it on fire. How did they know where she lived? That still remains as a secret! There were many others who suffered the same fate that night. We never imagined our own countrymen could be so cruel. That wasn't a war. It was genocide, and no one was there to protect us or do anything about it.

We were awake all night and did not know if the army would return that day. I had to go back to look for my father's hat because we wanted to get the missing piece of his skull. When I found it, I dug a hole and I buried in the spot where he had been shot. When I was done, I heard a big bomb. I piled stones on the burial site and hoped it would be enough to the animals from digging it out.

I ran back to the house because the bombing had gotten more intense in the other village. The army encountered some resistance from the rebel forces, and a helicopter was bombing the village. We didn't know if the helicopter would come to our village. We were not prepared for more destruction, and we had three bodies to bury.

Some of the men had managed to escape, but we didn't know where they were. The carpenter in the village made caskets of all sizes. Was he dead or alive? If he was still alive, where could we find him? Was his house still standing?

My mother decided to send my older sister and me away because the bombs were falling near our village. She gave us her blessings and told us that she needed to save us because we were her only young ones. She was not going to run the risk of losing us too. Drenched in tears, we went to hide with my mom's cousins who lived in a village that hadn't been affected yet.

We grabbed whatever we could and began our journey into the unknown, leaving behind everything. We did not know if we were going to see each other again. I stood in front of the gate and said goodbye to my father for the last time. We left at nine in the morning and followed the creek until it ran into a river. We could still see the bombs coming down. We didn't think anyone who had been left behind would survive.

We didn't know if we should try to save ourselves or go back. It was not an easy choice. The troops were surrounding the last members of our family. We were fatherless already, and if the bombs were dropped on the rest of my family, what were we supposed to do? My sister was crying, and she couldn't bear the thought of being an orphan.

That extraordinary strength wrapped around me again. I was able to console my sister and carry on with our journey. The trail wasn't an easy one. It had mountains, rocks, and barbed wire. We made it in one piece, but it was about three on the afternoon. My mother's cousin didn't even know we were coming. We told him everything and asked to stay with him until my mother and the rest of the family showed up for us.

We were worried because the situation at home had

not been resolved. It was going to be another sleepless night for us. How could we sleep when we didn't know if our family was still alive? I thought we were there for a reason. Our lives were not finished yet. We were going to make it. I kept preaching to myself and to my sister.

The next morning, we were anxious to hear of my family's fate. My mom had told us not to leave my uncle's place, but not knowing what had happened back at our house was torture. My uncle lived in a secluded area near a river. The next house was almost an hour away. Nobody wanted to risk going to a place that been bombed. Our only option was waiting until my mother came for us.

The helicopter didn't make it to our village, but the neighboring village was completely destroyed. People were killed, houses were burned, and all the crops and livestock were damaged. Those who had hidden in the mountains were caught in the middle of the fight. Two relatives, including a teenage girl, were raped and murdered.

The people who managed to escape returned to see what was left of their possessions. The carpenter and his house had been spared. My mother contacted my sister who lived in town and told her about our situation in a discrete manner, fearing the townspeople who were involved in the death squads. My sister was to make things look as normal as possible and not raise any suspicions. She was to hold the pain of losing her father inside and pretend that everything was all right. She and my mother started to work a plan simultaneously without communicating with each other. There was only one-way communication. The people who had managed to escape didn't want to go back to the village, but that was the only way the news spread.

One of our relatives lived in the big city and worked in a funeral home. My sister ordered three caskets. She knew it was going to be a challenge to transport the caskets to the village, but she would do the impossible and bring the caskets so my father and uncles could be buried like human beings. The carpenter took the measurements and used the lumber my father had cut for the doors of our new house.

They hauled the lumber about six kilometers to his shop. He was working against the clock. Using only hand tools, he was putting the caskets together not knowing that my sister was bringing them.

My sister and her crew had to carried the three caskets over the mountain and then down to the valley where we lived. The sun had gone down, and they were at least fifteen kilometers away from where the funeral vehicle had dropped the three caskets. It was not easy to carry the caskets at night with a small number of people.

My mother found some volunteers to dig a mass grave on our empty lot beside our house. She didn't surrender to adversity. She picked the spot where she was going to place her beloved husband of forty years and the father of her nine children. It was her final moment with him, and she apologized to him because she couldn't give him a better burial. It was the best she could do under the circumstances. She was doing everything possible to leave him in a safe place where he no longer had to worry about his family.

When news arrived that my sister was coming with the three caskets, a messenger told the carpenter to stop working on the caskets because we were not going to need them. It was great news for the carpenter since it was no fun to be working on such an enormous task.

My sister was anxious to see the site and help my mom finalize the burial. My mother and the rest of my sisters were relieved to know that help was on the way—and that the chapter was going to close soon.

My sister made it with the three caskets late that night, and there was nothing they could do but wait until morning to continue with the burial. The grave had yet to be finalized since there were not many who could excavate an enormous grave for three bodies with a pick and shovel. On the third day, they had to say goodbye to the man who had died for his beloved family. He knew they were capable of killing us all if they didn't find him at home that night, and he didn't want us to be slaughtered. He decided to die instead of us, and he voluntarily walked toward the creek where he was executed.

On the afternoon of the third day, they managed to put everything together. A small number of people brought the bodies to the grave. The day was coming to an end, and there was nothing left for them to stay for. Where would we go from there? The man who had everything figured it out was gone, and our mom was going to pick up the torch to light the way for us.

In the morning, my sisters looked around for the last time, said goodbye to their beloved father, and went to find my sister and me. My mother's final goodbye was yet to come. Three days passed without word from us, and she was worried. My grandparents had to be moved as well. Even our livestock and pets were left behind.

That afternoon, we were reunited at my uncle's house. Only two of my sisters had accompanied my mother because the other had gone back to town. She took the responsibility to set the stage to move forward.

On the fourth morning, she told me to get ready because we were going back to see if we could save some of what was left. I don't know how she managed to contact a wealthy man who lived near her cousin and get him to meet us there.

He had offered to buy all our pigs, and we were to hurry since the man was on horseback. My sisters didn't want to go back, but a cousin offered her help. The three of us had to find a way to save all the merchandise that didn't catch fire—plus all our chickens, two cats, my horse, and a few cattle my father had released the night he was murdered.

When we got there, the animals were loose and hungry. They all ran toward us, and it was heartbreaking to see the cats so hungry. There was nothing I could do since I was in the same situation. We gathered some of the grains and fed the animals. We had to decide what we were going to do with them.

While mom was negotiating with the man, I spent a few minutes at my father's grave. I tried to cry but something didn't let me. All I could feel was desolation. In the village, there were just a few people left, and they were planning to leave. The man was going to buy as much as possible and come back with his men to pick it up.

A man from the other village asked how many people in my family had been murdered. I didn't know what he was doing there until I saw a number of men coming toward us with guns. He introduced himself as a commander of the rebel forces, and he was recruiting people to join their forces. They were going to the soccer field for training. I was not afraid of them. He talked to me about the situation and told me that it was my chance to avenge the death of my father. He said, "I'm here to train you." He put a nine-millimeter gun in my hand and told me to get ready to fight for justice.

Without hesitation, I said, "Nothing will bring my father back, and I'm a Christian, which means that I can't go around killing people."

The man wasn't supposed to give me a choice. In those days, young people had no choice but to join the army or the rebel forces. He carried on with his training, and I watched for a few minutes. I said goodbye to the commander and walked away like I was the one in charge, and he didn't object.

I had been talking with one of the commanders of the rebel forces, but something kept me shielded from getting involved in anything but my ministry. I was being preserved for something much better than being a rebel or government soldier. When I was face-to-face with the member of the death squad, I was left untouched. The man patted my shoulder and told me to get out of the house because he was going to set it on fire. When I went outside, it was like I wasn't there for him and the other men who had my father at gunpoint. They didn't kill me because something that didn't let them.

We still had a lot of merchandise left over, and mom gave it to some of the people who were around. Some were going to stay because they had nowhere else to go, and some had land and possessions they were trying to hang on to. It wasn't hard to get rid of the things we couldn't carry, and everybody there needed something.

As we left our beloved village, we closed the only door of our house that had been left standing. For the last time, the door that had protected us was closed forever. We had no intention of returning. We were homeless and fatherless. From that point on, we had to figure it out where to go and what to do. Mom was in charge, and we trusted that she was going to lead us to a new place to have a house and rebuild our lives. Although our possessions were only those we were able to carry, we had each other.

We were going to make it together. With that attitude, we began our journey. Although we didn't know the meaning of it, God was in control—and He was not going to abandon us.

July 4 is a day I will never forget, but I could see God's hand working on our behalf. Although things didn't happen the way I would have liked them to happen, I was able to see God's presence the entire time. From the time those men got to my house to the moment I awoke into the world of the homeless, I found myself facing the reality of having nothing. Why God didn't intervene in my father's death is a question I cannot answer, but His presence was shown in a mighty way.

The rain came just in time to put out the fire in our house, and the thunder sounded like more than thunder. To escape untouched was something that could only happen by the hand of God. It was like God made me invisible. With the exception of the soldier who had ask me to get out because he was going to set the house on fire. For the other two soldiers who had my father on the ground, they walked around me with their rifles on their shoulders like I wasn't there.

The commander of the rebel army—and God—gave me the opportunity to escape by just saying no. His mission was to recruit people who had lost members of their families. Many of the teenagers who managed to escape from the army were trapped by the rebels. Many didn't make it to their twenties. That could have been me if I had taken that road.

Ever since my encounter with Jesus, I knew He had a purpose for my life. His presence always pointed me to the right direction. Even if I walked through the valley of death, I knew I was going to come out alive on the other side. I don't understand why everything else happened the way it happened, but I chose to trust God. He knows the reasons why He allowed them to happen.

CHAPTER 9

A Week after We Buried the Dead

We often use the word *nightmare* when we go through a horrible situation, when something bad happens to us, or when we have a bad dream. What about if the nightmare itself were a safe place where you could find refuge and prefer not to be awakened? You feel somehow that it's better to stay there than to come out into the real world!

There are times in life when everything seems like it is a nightmare. You go to sleep thinking that it will be gone by the morning, but while you sleep, you are reliving the moment you were victimized. From your subconscious comes a loud scream for help, but you still are being denied the help human beings deserve. When you wake up, the nightmare hasn't finished yet. The real world is even worse than your nightmare because everything you had or the one thing you loved the most is gone forever. You see the past, but you can't conceive of a future without the thing that made you whole. You feel abandoned by society. You are there—but it would be better if you weren't. You feel like society has turned its back on you because it no longer feels the needs of other human beings.

One week after we returned from my village for the last time, I found myself among relatives I hardly knew. We were not planning to stay there for long, but while my mother figured it out, we stayed in a place where one more person was too many. The people were nice, and they tried to accommodate us. Unfortunately, their residence could not handle many people.

My mother and three of my sisters were trying to put everything behind them. My mother was doing everything possible to get us back on the road. She was not going to wait until our supplies and money ran out. We had to move fast and find a solution to our problem. There was no way we would return for our crops. We were not going to take any chances and wait around in that battleground. It was hard to leave our crops behind. The rebel forces took over the village, and the real battle began.

Something horrible had happened, but it didn't hit me like it hit my mom and my siblings. Even when I tried to cry, I couldn't. I felt a force within me that didn't let me cry. It was like my body was there, but my spirit was somewhere that pain didn't exist. During those moments, I was able to comfort everyone—even the little kids who were so frightened. Some of the three-year-old got down on their knees and prayed to God for help. I knew then that God had prepared me to minister to my people during the darkest night. I knew God was with me, but I didn't know to what extent. There was no chance that I would be alive if it wasn't for God. He had put a cloak of protection over me.

A week later, God revealed Himself in a peculiar way to let me know I had not been alone. He confirmed to me that His Word is true when He said, "I will uphold you with my righteous right hand." He showed me how he had held me in His hand—and that was why I was still alive.

Some cousins were going to take me fishing at night. The river was about a block away, and we had to get harpoons ready. We were going for shrimp, and we needed some clothe hangers, wood, and rubber strings for the harpoons.

At six o'clock, it was dark already. The cousins tried to help me forget my tragedy and move on with my life. I had a wonderful time fishing with the guys, and it seemed that all had been left in the past. I was making a smooth transition to my new life. The fishing went very well, and we managed to catch three or four pounds of shrimp in a couple of hours. We came back to the house and prepared the shrimp for the next day. I thought I could integrate into that lifestyle. I was trying to convince myself that it wasn't so bad. I didn't know I was living under the covering God put on me to survive the tragedy. I had to face reality and learn how to deal with the fact that everything was going to be different.

In the morning, something was different. It was like I had been let go into a deep hole, and there wasn't any escape. I felt like I had been abandoned in the middle of nowhere and was surrounded by ferocious beasts. I made my way to a huge rock in the front lot, and I climbed it and began to cry like a baby.

I awakened from the nightmare I had been living in, but I was coming out of that safe place within. My eyes were opened. I could see everything that had happened, and I was feeling the pain in my own flesh. I never question God. I knew I was alone.

I sat in a fetal position, and God's voice came to me it was my time to mourn. For the past week, he had been holding me in His arms. That was why no one could harm me. I had been under His protection all the way. He was lifting the veil so I could see His mighty power and trust Him. He was going to be with me wherever I went, but it was necessary for me to grieve my father's death.

I felt something big and heavy coming out of me, and then I felt empty. I heard my two cousins calling me, and when I didn't answer, they came to find me. "It is okay to cry, cousin. You need to get rid of all that pain." They let me know I was not alone. It was a confirmation of the promise of God that I was not alone. Although things looked cloudy, I didn't have to worry. He had chosen me to live long past my teen years.

After that time of solitude with God, I began to move into a different phase of my life. I have had another personal encounter with God. I saw His mighty hand tilted toward me. It was like a powerful giant was protecting me and my heart. If I had escaped from that attack, would it have been possible to experience the favor of God in that same manner?

Although I had lost everything with the exception of my mother and siblings, I never thought the promise of God would fail me. Was I afraid? Yes, but that never stopped me from doing what I was called to do.

I moved from place to place, fully trusting God for my protection—even when I had to go through dangerous places. I learned to fully depend on God for everything, and I knew that I had it all—even when I didn't have an inch of land to call my own. Although I could only see empty possibility ahead of me, God had promised to look after me.

He was letting me feel the pain like the rest of all my family, but it was going to be over soon. Sixteen years of age qualified me to join the government army or the rebels. The rebels had risen from the hurt people who had lost their families. I was perfect for becoming a soldier to their army, and that put my mother on the edge of death. She was extremely concerned. No one was safe anywhere. I was risking my life every time I moved from one place to another. If I went somewhere, I could get caught in the crossfire, be recruited to serve in the army, or be taken by rebel forces. I was I afraid all the time because it wasn't on my list to go into an army and fight a fight I never believed in.

I memorized verses that gave me confidence that I was going to make it. One of those verses was Romans 8:31, and I needed a lot of confidence because my future was uncertain. When I tried to look into my future, I couldn't see how I was going to make it on my own.

As I climbed down off the rock, I felt like a piece of me was missing. I summarized the week prior to my father's death and meditated on the final moments we spent together. I understood then that he was trying to protect me during those nights of hiding in the woods. The last two nights, we were cold and wet from the dew after sleeping on rocks under thorny trees full of burning ants.

Those were not the greatest nights, but when the morning came, we had each other. Now there was a big void in me. It was like a part of me was gone. I asked the Lord why I was feeling like that, and He told me it was okay to feel empty inside because I had just separated from the only man who He had set on this earth to care for me. It was time to fully trust Him, and He took over. I didn't have to worry about my future.

I didn't understand what God was trying to do or say, but I believed Him and began to walk toward the house. My mother noticed something was different with me, but I didn't know how to explain what had happened on that rock. God had revealed what had happened, but I couldn't explain to my mother why I was feeling different. I knew it was my responsibility to care for my mother and my little sister since the rest of my siblings were dispersed. We still didn't know what had happened to some of them. After being a united family, we all had to go in different directions. Our foundation had collapsed, and it was not possible to put it back together again.

When I woke up from my nightmare, I learned that it was time to look into my future. I felt like I had been sleeping and was waking up in a different world. I knew no one there, but I had been told not to fear. He owned the past and the future.

My experience with the Almighty had been real, but I still felt a sense of abandonment. It wasn't easy to see myself in the future—even after I had seen the hand of God protecting me. I knew there were many trials ahead of me, but I wasn't far from the place where I had lost everything.

With nothing left, I had to face the unknown and rely only on the promise of the invisible God that had told me not to fear. He was going with me everywhere I went.

CHAPTER 10

Shot at Close Range

He shall cover thee with his feathers,
and under his wings shalt thou trust: his
truth shall be thy shield and buckler.

—Psalm 91:4

In order to know if something is there, we must see it or touch it. Sometimes faith doesn't kick in until there is no way out. We close our eyes and call upon God's protection. In our human nature, we always struggle when it comes to fully depending on the provision of God. He said that He would be there in any circumstance. He is working in our favor—or at least the way we want to see things—or He is working in the opposite way of our own understanding.

It is challenging to have childlike faith and say, "Lord, I won't be afraid. I won't dismay because I trust you."

That would be the correct way for all believers, but humans always have negative thoughts coming to our minds. When we don't see things as God said they would be or when we are constantly harassed by adversity, it seems like we can't see the end. Sometimes we feel like we're walking in a minefield. Regardless of how we walk, our lives will still be in danger. Danger is everywhere, and no matter how carefully we conduct ourselves, there is always the possibility of falling into the snare.

Our walk with the Lord is amazing. God is exposing us to danger so we can see His presence and understand that we need to be in trouble to be rescued. We see His Word materializing because we went through the valley of death and managed to go right through it. That is when we have the opportunity to see God working on our behalf.

About three weeks after my father's death, my mother decided to get as far away from that region as possible. We had relatives in the western part of the country. It was ten hours by bus, but my mom thought we needed to give it a try. Since we had next to nothing to carry, it wasn't hard to make the trip.

We managed to get there the same day, but we were late. As we got there, we knew it was going to be hard to settle in. It was not going to be easy to forget everything and pretend nothing had happened. We had to act like we were the happiest people in the world.

Even though we were in the same country, we had landed in a totally different culture. We had to be cautious since it was the same country with the same problems. We thought everything was going to be all right since everybody looked nice. Everyone was doing their own thing. It was a prosperous village, and most villagers had farms. Some of them were coffee growers, and there was a big de-pulping plant at the top of the mountain. They produced corn, beans, rice, cattle, and honey, and they were busy all year round.

I was fortunate to arrive in a place with the same characteristics as the place where I had been born. It didn't take long to settle down and lease five acres of land so I could have it ready for the following year. I found work with the locals for the remaining part of the year and a place of worship close to where I was staying.

My mission was to support my mother and my little sister since my other siblings had gone in different directions. I thought it wouldn't be difficult to support myself and two others, and I began to work for relatives and other locals. The coffee plantations were where the money was.

I made good money picking coffee beans. They used to pay between ₡1.50 and ₡2.25 for every twenty-five-pounds of ripe coffee beans. Harvest was from November until January, and we were in good shape for Christmas. We had money to buy new clothes and new shoes for Christmas. My first six months were very nice. I managed to make friends, and I was neighbors with relatives I had not visited very often.

In the last six months of 1980, my life had changed. The tragedy had made me mature quickly, and my mother was constantly praying for me. I felt a sense of security and protection.

Within a month, my mother found a house for rent. As a blessing, the rent was next to nothing. The pastor from the village decided to move to another house and asked my mother if she wanted to move into his house. All we needed to do was take care his beehives. It wasn't much to do since bees take care for themselves most of the time, but he needed someone to feed them during the dry season and protect them from army ants. He had thirty beehives, and from November until the end of March, my job was to feed the bees by diluting brown sugar in water and putting it on top of their wooden boxes. My other job was to be ready with pesticide. When the army ants came, I had to spray around the stands. The army ants would conduct a total search to the area twice a year, and when that happened, it was devastated. They would cover more than a kilometer each time, killing all insects and small animals, including snakes. Beehives were their favorite for the honey and for the larvae.

The pastor trained me for the job. I knew when the ants would invade the area, and I had to be on watch all the time. The episodes would occur during the day, and that was my plus in that situation. I also paid attention to the birds. When the ants were coming, the birds were right behind them. The birds were catching all the insects that were trying to escape from the ants. That was my number one sign.

The first time it happened, I ran to see what was happening. I saw the ants approaching the beehives. It was amazing to see millions of small creatures covering every square inch of a square block. The bees wouldn't stand a chance against the ants. That was why the pastor couldn't leave them unattended. His new home was about a day away by bus. He was pastoring two churches, and he had to commute every week between the churches. When I went to work for the locals, my mother took charge of the situation. That was how we paid our rent.

From August until December, I took my first steps on my own. I knew I couldn't replace my father, and I had to carry on. I went forward but it was not possible to avoid looking back. When I felt down, I wished I could go back in time and change what had happened. My heart wasn't completely healed, but God gave me hope.

Nonetheless, I felt like my heart was going to come out of my chest, I ran into a cornfield. The corn was high enough that no one could see me. I felt like nothing was going right for me. I had more questions than answers, and there was no one who could help me. In that moment of desperation, I looked around and found myself alone in the world. I went back to the past and then to my future. I couldn't make it on my own. I was trying to figure out what to do with this monumental load on my shoulders. I was broken and in tears. I felt like nothing could replace what I had lost. There was this emptiness within me, and I didn't know how to deal with it.

Broken in spirit and having no one to turn to, I lifted my eyes to heaven and screamed with my heart to the one who had promised me that He would not leave me alone. With uncontainable tears in my eyes, I told the Lord that He was going to be my heavenly Father—and I needed Him to be my earthly father too. I spent time meditating about what I had asked. For a moment, I thought what I said was crazy. After all, it was just me there. Nobody else had heard me. I felt the need to go down on my knees and continue the conversation with the Lord.

I began to feel the sweet presence of the Counselor coming down on and reassuring me that there was no right or wrong in how we call onto God. It gave me the assurance that I had been heard by my heavenly Father. My request had been granted even before I had made it. I don't know how long I spent there in conversation with God, but after I finished, I wasn't the same person. All the burden and emptiness had disappeared, and I was no longer the same. I was no longer fatherless. I had a sense of security. I could count on someone who was not going to desert me. I took that as an answer to my prayer. I could hang on to the promise of God and not rely on my feelings. He had promised that nothing was going to stand in my way. I had to trust Him.

I looked around to see if anyone had heard me. Anyone listening at me would think I was out of this world. That didn't matter to me. When I got out of that place, I wasn't the same. I had seen my future and had been given assurance that everything was going to be all right. After that, I felt like a giant emotionally.

I looked for my mother, but I never told her where I had been or what I had been doing. For some reason, I never shared my experiences with anyone—not even my mother. Perhaps I didn't know how to communicate my personal experiences with her because she was my mom. Maybe I was afraid of confusing her while trying to explain something that would give her the impression that I was depressed.

I always pretended to be the strongest one during our crises because after losing all we had, she felt so much emotional distress. When she went by police or soldiers, she would start shaking uncontrollably. That was one of the reasons I tried to keep things hidden from her. It was my job to keep her safe. I also tried to hide my pain from her. I knew it would break her heart if she saw me crying or struggling to cope with what was going on.

In that moment of desperation, I ran into that field because I couldn't handle it anymore. I had to release that anxiety and ask God for help. I didn't have a psychologist or a counselor who could help me cope with my loss. I had to try to go deeper into the spiritual world and reach out to the Lord because I didn't know what else to do. I am glad I did because I never had another episode like that.

I felt the presence of God coming to my assistance—and it has never left.

During that transitional time, my real test began. I had come to a place where I hardly knew the locals, and I was still just a boy with nothing to offer. For people to take me seriously, I had to be at least eighteen. That was the part that didn't sink in. How was it going to be possible to support myself and my family? Perhaps God was giving me more than I could handle. Maybe I had forgotten who He was and did not realize He hadn't forgot me.

When things are going well, it is easy to say, "I love you Jesus." At least there is something to eat, and there is food for tomorrow. It is not as easy when you are wearing your last pair of pants and shoes—and you don't know how you will cover the basic necessities.

I could not go to a bank for a loan or get social assistance while I got back on my feet. No one knew me, and I had nothing to offer. My biggest possession was the clothes I was wearing. When I thought there was nothing left for me, God showed me He had never left me. He had kept me standing. Why wasn't I trusting Him? From that moment on, all my fears were gone. I began to see how the hand of God was protecting me. I could see His grace upon me everywhere I went.

It wasn't a random chance that I went into that field that day. It was a special moment to spend time before my heavenly Father. He called me to make me feel loved by Him. In that moment, I felt His arms embracing me. He was calling me His child. In the breeze, I could feel His presence filling the entire place. With that kind of power over me, it was clear that I had conquered all my fears. From that point forward, I was going to be able to see His protection over me. I never questioned why I would need extra protection if I had come to a place where everybody was nice. I was content to have God watching over me.

In the final months of 1980, everything was calm. I left my struggles behind, and I was moving in a great direction. My new village was full of great things for me. I found peace, and some of the villagers were helping me grow by teaching me some of their skills. Skills were needed to progress, become a farmer, and own land.

War in that place was out of the question. No one was preoccupied with what was going on in the rest of the country. Everybody was busy working their lands. The village was between towns, but there was only one exit for vehicles to move the produce. I decided to move forward with my own crops. I made a deal with one of the villagers and reserved a piece of land for my crops.

I spent the first three months of the following year working for farmers and coffee growers. In the spring, I would start my own thing. I had great expectations. The land I reserved was some of the best. I had found favor before the farmer, and he told me he was going to give me the piece of land in front of his house. It was one of his best pieces of land. He was not going to charge me anything for that season, and he was going to give me the two types of seeds I needed. It didn't surprise me. I knew the grace of God was upon me. The man explained in detail to how much that land should produce. He calculated every square meter in pounds, and it was a great relief to find someone who was able to trust me and give me a chance to start my career as a farmer. I worked hard that spring to get the land ready. I also worked for him to show my appreciation for what he was doing for me.

In the spring, I was ready to carry on with my project. Before I knew it, my crops were coming. Something from my imagination had materialized, and I was excited about my accomplishments. I worked hard to keep up with my field and help my relatives who were in the same business. Caring for crops was more difficult than I thought it would be. After three weeks, my green beans were hit by a plague. It was devouring it all.

My landlord had all kinds of knowledge about that situation. He provided me with the right pesticide, which worked great, and my enthusiasm grew even bigger. I couldn't wait for the harvest. When the second quarter came to an end, it was harvest time. By then, I had an idea how my production was going to be. I had done everything I had been told, and I was hoping for the best return. I had followed all the instructions from my landlord, and he was positive that I would get what he normally did from that piece of land.

I had been watching the development of my beans and corn. They had grown nice and healthy, and their foliage was enough to fool anyone about what was going on underneath. Although the plants had grown properly, there was not enough fruit for each plant. I kept trusting the landlord, thinking I couldn't go wrong. I didn't want to say anything before it was time, but I was kind of confused about what I was seeing.

It meant a lot to me. It was my first time doing something so big on my own. I felt it was a test and thought I could do it alone. For years, I had been working under my father's watch, and now I had to prove that I was ready to face my future. My neighbors were doing well, and I thought I had I chance to grow and become established in my new village.

The village had everything I needed to be successful. There were all kinds of things that could be done besides farming. One of the most important factors for the economy of that sector was the coffee plantations. They benefited the entire community. People from other countries were farming all kinds of fruits to export to North America, and it was easy to find work or get involved in something that would produce an income.

I really liked my new village. I lived beside the church and the main road that was used to bring produce to town. It seemed like I had found my new home. I had no plans to move because everything I needed was there.

The time came to pick my crops, something I was relying on, and I felt proud because I had been able to make it on my own. It was my sustenance for part of the year. My landlord went into the field to check on the beans because it was getting close to harvest time. He wanted to give me an idea about when I should start to pick them, and he was disappointed after he saw that my beans had almost gone to waste. They had grown but produced almost nothing. The bushes had grown, but there was not much to pick from the plants. He was disappointed because the land had been wasted for the season. There was nothing he could do since I had followed his farming techniques. His only question was why.

I was concerned because of the great monetary loss. He had calculated that those acres of land should produce a thousand pounds of beans. It had shrunk to two hundred pounds, which I couldn't afford. Something else concerned me more. It had something to do with my identity. Although I didn't question myself at the moment because I wanted to give it another try, soon enough, the answer was clear to me. I had focused on getting on with what I thought I had to do to earn a living, and I had forgotten that the Lord had told me He was going to be there for me. I had forgotten that I was His child. He had called me to do what He knew was best for me. I had started the career I thought was best for me. Had God called me to be a farmer?

During that season, I felt lost without knowing who I really was. I couldn't see beyond what my eyes could see, but I knew the Lord was shaping me into the person who He wanted me to be. Without resentment against God,

I began to ask Him what was next for me. If I had been brought to that new place, what was my assignment?

Shortly after that, I began to engage in my ministry of witnessing Christ to the people in my new community. There were not many people attending church. It was mostly the pastor's family and his in-laws. The rest of the villagers didn't want anything to do with the church. I had the opportunity to share the Gospel with some of the villagers who I believed were touched by the Holy Spirit, and that was what God had called me to do. I had been called to tell people the great news that everyone needed to hear. I felt freedom when I was delivering the message of salvation to those who didn't know Jesus, but at the moment, I couldn't understand God's plans.

I finished picking my crops and went to work for the locals while I got ready for the next season. Everything looked good, and it seemed like I had found peace in that place. No one was talking about the war that was going on in the rest of the country. Even my sister who had stayed in the town near my home village used to spend time with us. She never lost sight of my mother and the rest of us. She gave most of her earnings to my mother so we wouldn't go hungry. I had great respect for my sister. She worked hard for the well-being of all her siblings. She was the big sister to all of us, and when the time to decide came, her word was heard. When she dropped by to see our mom, it was delightful to have her. She usually visited for just a week. When she had to go back to town, it was a full day of traveling by bus.

I was absolutely happy. I had a place to live and a place to work. I thought my future there was going to be wonderful. I might not be a farmer, but I would be doing something that God would approve of. If I ministered in the church, I could take the Gospel to those who were not part of the Evangelical community. There was also the possibility of going to a Bible seminary to prepare myself to serve God in the ministry. The community needed ordained pastors who would take the challenge of building the community in true Christianity. There was the need to prepare more people who were willing to take the Gospel further than it had been taken. A large group had yet to be reached. I knew they were also in the heart of God. He wanted them to understand His Son, and He knew what was in the near future for many of them.

A few months went by, and war was more evident in the surrounding areas. There were many villages divided by mountains and farmland, and we could see them from long distances. Some of those villages were from other jurisdictions that were governed by the same military system. Sometimes they didn't share the information right away, and in some cases, that would allow people to escape persecution.

I was happy that I had found a new home in that village, and it never crossed my mind that I was going to run into the same fate as I had in my home village. That was in the past, and I had stepped into a new place that I could call home. I thought nobody would make me leave again.

Helicopters started hammering faraway villages, and we could see the smoke through the mountains. The army had encountered resistance in those villages, and the fight had taken place on *El Cerro de Guazapa*. The heroes—the defenders of the people—were fighting the rebels, and the army was gaining control of the villages that were under control of the rebel forces—at least those were the reports we heard. I couldn't believe it. I knew exactly what was happening to those villages. It felt like I was reliving my past, which didn't make sense to me.

My heart trembled at the thought of going through that ordeal again, especially when I thought I had found a safe refuge. Everybody was confident that our village was protected from harm. No one was paying attention to what was happening in the surrounding area except the people who had come from other places.

My mother began to fear for my life since I was the only son who was around. She was protecting me like an endangered species, and we began praying. This time, we had to do things differently. Our experiences with the war had taken us to a different level than the rest of the villagers, and even if we wanted to make them aware of the danger, it was something we couldn't explain. It was hard to see all those people who had no idea how war could change their lives in an instant.

It was devastating to think about the beauty of that

place coming to an end. Human lives that were at risk—even when there was no motive for them to kill. They would face no consequences. They were cruel people who could not care less about anyone young or old. Once they got to these places, everything was ruined. I couldn't imagine seeing the daily lives of those people turning to mourning or death. Perhaps some of them would suffer the same fate as the baker who came every morning with a big basket as big as he was. He used to supply the villagers with bread, and every family was ready every morning—seven days a week—for his bread. Bent to the ground with that huge basket, he would travel along the main road and bring people something to enjoy at the beginning of the day. He had to start very early to make it on time for everybody. He didn't show up one day. Everybody got up at the usual time and waited for him. Instead, he was lying dead under the coffee trees with his basket by his side. The road he had traveled thousands of times had witnessed a crime that was the norm for a country that had no laws against its supposed security forces. Once again there was another crime that had gone to impunity.

I knew things were getting bad, and it was time to seek refuge elsewhere. The question was where. I tried to keep my mother calm. I thought God would provide a way for us to avoid the same calamity. I was going to work as usual—but not with the same enthusiasm. For the locals, losing their baker was not going to change their way of living. They only thought bad things happened to good people, and they never imagined that their village was about to change. No one could take his place because it required strength and passion. We all missed that morning treat, but no one paid attention to the signs of what was coming.

The days went by, and I almost forgot that I should have been looking for new alternatives instead of staying there until tragedy struck again. It all seemed normal. The locals were tending to their fields and looking forward to a great harvest.

One day, as we were working close by my boss's house, helicopters and bombers flew overhead. I panicked and thought, *This is it.*

Fortunately for me, the airplanes were on a mission to level a village that was about twenty kilometers away from where we were standing. The army went to a village named *El Bogote*, lined up the men, women, and children, and shot them all with a machine gun. The media was not talking about the massacre. A few people who managed to escape explained what had happened to their community. There were not even enough people left alive to bury the dead. All the bodies were left to rot. According to the few who escaped, they were not able to go back because of the constant surveillance.

I spoke with a man who had a relative in that village, and he told me that they couldn't go back because the army was watching. Wild animals and dogs were feeding on the corpses. I was able to see vultures flying over the village, and that was proof that what these people were saying was the truth. I was sure I had to leave my place of refuge, but I had to work on the logistics and wait to see what God's plan was.

During that period, my big sister had come to spend some time with us. She had moved to the capital to be closer to us, and she was planning to stay a little longer than usual. We were all happy to have her with us, especially my mother, and I forgot what was going on in our surroundings. I kept on doing my usual work in the fields and going to church, and I was not thinking about the future.

After a hard day of work, I went home for dinner and went to sleep early. That way, I could get up fully energized in the morning. That was my routine during weekdays. I had to wait until Sunday for church or to go to the city. There was nothing else to do in the evening. I was oblivious to the fact that danger was imminent. As people who had gone through so much in the past year, I should have been more vigilant about what was happening.

One day, it pleased the Lord to show me my future—just a few hours ahead—and then my present so I could have an idea of what was coming. A few weeks after the massacre in *El Bogote*, the unexpected happened to our village. Something had been brewing, but none of us knew that everything was about to change for everybody in the village. I had not much to lose, but for the rest of the villagers, that place was everything. The order of the things that followed remains a mystery to me, but I learned to trust God in any circumstance.

It was the middle of the week, and we all were making plans for the weekend. We would have some fun, have a nice family dinner, and show my sister some appreciation. I went to sleep that night thinking about how much fun it was going to be. I slept until five the following morning. I usually got up around six, but I was woken up an hour early by a vision. The Lord showed me what was happening during that hour while I was still on bed. The army was surrounding my boss's house where all the workers gathered every morning around seven. I was to be at that house at seven since I was scheduled to be in the crew for the day. He showed me the soldiers who were hiding in the bushes along a barbed wire fence along the property line. The property was fenced all around and measured twenty or twenty-five hectares. Most of it was used to grow corn and beans. A steep hill with a small channel at the bottom collected water during the rainy season. In the vision, I saw myself running from the soldiers. I was quicker than them and got away by going under a fence that they couldn't jump or go under. The fence started from the main road and went down the hill. The corn and beans were high enough to cover an average person. Anybody could hide in the trees along the fences on both sides of the property.

After the vision, I found myself on my knees. I asked the Lord for an explanation. I was trembling. The run had seemed so real, and my heart was beating faster than ever. I prayed that morning and asked God to show me what He really meant in the vision. "Will I be chased by these soldiers, Lord?" I asked. I never heard God talking back to me in that moment, but I knew He was listening to me. I trusted that, whatever happened, I was going to be all right.

I got up, but I didn't want to say anything to anyone—not even my mother. I had breakfast and went to work, which was only ten or fifteen minutes away. When I got there, everything appeared to be normal, but I was still living the moment from the vision. I couldn't get it out of my mind. It felt so real that I looked around for anything suspicious. I didn't see anything besides guys having coffee. I thought I should have seen signs, but that wasn't the case.

Maybe God was showing me something in the far future—or something not necessarily in the same order I had seen it. I never had the courage to tell the guys what was on my mind. Since none of them were believers, I didn't want them to ridicule me.

When the full crew got together, all seven of us, we went to the bean fields. We walked about five hundred meters, about halfway down the hill, and two men stopped us. They said they were from *El Bogote* and hadn't eaten a proper meal for three weeks. They confirmed the rumors we had heard about the massacre and asked my boss for work.

My boss was touched by their story and hired them on the spot. He said, "Go up. I will let my wife know you are on the way. She will give you something to eat so you can come to work for me."

While we were talking to these men, we heard someone yelling from the other side of the fence. A group of soldiers was hiding about fifteen meters away from us, and we had no clue we were being watched all along.

About six soldiers were aiming heavy weapons at us.

The commander shouted, "Stop! All of you, lift up your hands and come toward us."

I turned to the crew to see their reaction, and they were already down on the ground. They started rolling toward the creek and breaking through the corn. I didn't hesitate to do the same. It was a spontaneous reaction like we were programmed to do that.

Failing to obey the commander's orders triggered a negative reaction, and the soldiers began shooting at us with all the firepower they had. Now we were nine of us trying to escape, but we had no idea where to run. We spread out in different directions, but we had been surrounded.

At the top of another hill, soldiers came down and ambushed us. We had no chance to escape. They wanted to kill all of us. The shooting was so loud that I thought it was the end for me. The Lord reminded me of the vision from that morning. I asked for forgiveness as I was rolling on the ground since I hadn't heeded His warning.

The shooting lasted twenty or twenty-five minutes, but I felt peace while I was crawling on the ground. I was not afraid of dying—even when the bullets were flying overhead. My trust was in God, and if He had allowed that to happen, He also knew how he was going to glorify Himself through it all. I never looked back when they were shooting, but I could hear the shouting and crying beside me.

The soldiers were chasing us along the fence, which was not far from where we were. There is no doubt in my mind that I am telling this story because there was a divine intervention. The soldiers had grenade launchers and high-powered rifles.

I managed to roll down to the trail and jumped in the creek. I had to jump the barbed wire fence that was only about a foot above the water, but if I stood up, I was going to be cut in half. I crawled under it, but then I couldn't crawl anymore because of the terrain. The terrain was to my advantage with big trees and big rocks to take cover.

I was going to run down the creek as fast as could.

One of the men from *El Bogote* was leading the way for me, and I just kept running after him. "Follow me," he said. "I know a place where we can go."

We ran for about two hours until we saw a shack on the outskirts of *El Bogote*. He was back with some of the refugees who had escaped the wrath of the army. Two or three families had gotten together in that small house and were hanging by a thread.

About an hour later, the other man from *El Bogote* arrived, but he had not been so fortunate. He was hit but refused to give up, and he did whatever he had to do to escape—even walking on one foot. His right calf had been blown up, but he made a tourniquet with his shirt and was able to walk for two more hours.

We had no clue what had happened to the rest of the crew, and I began to worry about the rest of the crew and my relatives who had been left behind. It would be too much to think none of the others had been hurt or killed. Those were the only possibilities since those people didn't believe in arresting anyone. They said, "We forgive your life—or we kill you." Those were the only two options.

When I thought of my mother and three sisters who were left behind, I was frightened. There was no way to communicate with them. It was far away, and there was no way of knowing if the army had left. The next thing was to wait until the next day and try to find out what had happened to my family and the rest of the crew.

Emotionally broken and with a mountain of uncertainty before me, I had no choice but to wait in the land of the dead to see what was going to happen next. With an empty stomach feeling it like it was stuck to my spine, I began to relive my past. I didn't even think about my faith in God at that point. I had lost sight of who I was among those people who had no hope. I felt like I had been abandoned. I didn't want to talk about God to those people. I was sure God had brought me there to show them there was something more to suffering.

At home, it was chaos. My mom had seen enough already, and she was not going to accept losing her son too. She had heard all the shooting, and she knew the soldiers were shooting at us.

The soldiers had searched my boss's house for weapons—as well as the neighbors' houses. All the villagers were held for questioning, and some of them were tortured right in front of everybody because they suspected them of having ties to the rebels. People were intimidated, and they didn't want to do anything that would make them more suspicious or give them a reason to think they were part of the antigovernment people. They had to wait for them to leave and then find out for themselves what had happened.

The ordeal lasted for more than four hours, and they were trying to find any reason to justify all the shooting. They tried to make people confess that they were hiding weapons. My mother and big sister were anxiously waiting for them to leave so they could begin the search for me. Pretending that they were crying because they were nervous for their presence—and not because their son and brother was possibly dead—my mother and big sister managed to hang on until the soldiers decided to leave. If they found out someone from that house was in the group the soldiers had shot, things would get really complicated. They would have to reveal my name and all my information, and as a result, it was possible that my mom and sisters would be linked to terrorism. Although my mother's credentials had been changed to that address, mine was still under my old jurisdiction. That would be enough for them to think I was a mercenary traveling throughout the country. Either way, it would look like I was fighting against the government forces or being trained. That was why no one could say anything. Getting mixed up in something like that could be fatal.

My mother and big sister went down the hill to see what had happened to the crew. They didn't know about the two men we had met. They were focused on finding out what had happened to me. Crying and calling my name, they searched the field for my body. They couldn't find me. Other people who had joined the search found the body of one of the crew members. That sparked a big rage and made them believe there were more bodies in the woods. They searched all over, thinking I had been hit and gone to die elsewhere.

Family members of the rest of the crew tried to find their own, but the rest of the crew managed to escape. Crying and brokenhearted, my mom and big sister returned home. They thought I might have been hit and was dead in the woods since the rest of the crew had been accounted for. I was the only one missing, and no one knew what had happened to me. I was missing, and they thought I was dead. They had to find me before nightfall. Searching for a dead body at night was impossible.

My mother couldn't bear the pain of losing her son, and she decided to leave. She thought she had to escape from that place before things got any worse. She grabbed my little sister and went to another village where it was safer. A large number of people were affected by the incident, and they took a two-hour walk through trails and grasslands to find refuge at the *finca de Don Pedro*.

They thought the army was going to come back and kill them all. My big sister decided it was best for my mother to leave immediately, and she was going to stay behind until she found out what had happened to me. I have no idea how my big sister managed to convince my mother to leave and leave her behind. It was dangerous for a young woman to be alone in that situation.

I think God used my sister to make the decision; it was no coincidence she decided to visit us at the same time the army came to destroy our village. The determination to stay behind until she found me dead or alive couldn't have come from her alone. She and my other sister spent the night anxiously waiting for the morning and hoping things would work out.

I was planning to go back to the village to see what had happened. I was in a place where 90 percent of the villagers had been killed. In my mind, there was a possibility that my family could have suffered the same fate. Since genocide had been committed throughout the country—with no consequences for the aggressors—it wouldn't have surprised me if they slaughtered the people in my new village.

I spent the night under the only bed in the house on a dirt floor. The number of people who had found refuge in it was more than what the house could accommodate. I couldn't sleep at all. In the morning, we were all afraid the army would show up at any moment. They had to be ready to flee. They told me I had to wait at least until ten o'clock that morning. They would send someone to lead me to another village so I could find my way home. The walk was going to take about three hours, and I had to be careful crossing the village.

People were scared of strangers coming to their villages, since some of them were government informants. If they saw something out of the ordinary, they would contact the army right away. The villagers where I had spent the night explained all those things and tried to disguise me as one of their own to avoid suspicions. They found a *sombrero* and a *machete* so people I met would think I was just a local working man. I think the sombrero was from a dead man, but it didn't matter to me. I had to make it home.

One of the men walked me to the main road. I was afraid and didn't know what was ahead. I walked on a road I had never walked. Nobody knew me, and I had to pretend to be from the area and watch out for the army. If I ran across the army, I was going to be in deep trouble. All I had for identification was my church membership card, and that was not going to prove anything to those madmen.

I walked and ran for two hours before I got to the church and our house. To my surprise, the house was still standing. No one was in it. The whole place was empty. Trusting in God that all was well, I continued walking through my village. I was anxious about where my family was.

I had to find someone at my boss's house, and I ran over to see who else had made it or if the rest had been killed. On my way there, I met some of the villagers who were still around. Unfortunately, they didn't know much about where most of the people had gone. All they knew was that the army had come by their houses and taken people with them. They also had killed some, but they didn't know how many. I knew they had left, and I ran to my boss's to find some answers. The story was repeating itself? I didn't mind that so much. All I wanted was to see my family and know they were all right.

When I got closer to the boss's house, I saw a woman in front of a wooden stove with a *tortilla* in her hand. The house was about two hundred meters from the main road, and I was able to see who was there. My big sister had spent the night there to hear what had happened to me. She didn't recognize me because of the way I was dressed. It didn't take long before she realized it was me.

She dropped the *tortilla*, shouted my name, and ran to meet me. We cried, and she began telling me what had happened. That was the first time I felt that amount of fraternal love coming from one of my siblings. After many years, I still remember that moment like it happened yesterday. She poured out her soul and told me she thought she was never going to see me again.

It was like the picture Jesus portrays in the parable of the prodigal son, but this time, it was a sister who thought she had lost her brother and found him again. She thought I was dead, and she was rejoicing that I was alive. She took me in and fed me—but I still had to go find my mother.

I had to walk for three hours to get where my mother was. I had no clue where *Don Pedro's finca* was, but I had to show myself to my mother and my other two sisters. My big sister had said, "Go and bring my mother tomorrow because I am taking all of you out of this miserable place over my grandpa's house."

My grandpa used to live in one of the big cities. I don't know how she found out that he had left the city and abandoned the house. My mother's father had left the country because of the war. He wasn't aware of our situation, but we knew it would be okay to move into his house.

I had to find my mom before she went insane from thinking I was dead. I had been missing for twenty-four hours. In her mind, I had been shot and died somewhere in the woods. She was completely devastated that no one had been able to find me. "At least find his body so I can bury him," she said.

This time I didn't have to worry much about the locals since it was most grassland and coffee plantations that I had to go through. After two and a half hours, I arrived at my destination. It was painful to find my mother and see how devastated she was. She hadn't eaten since the moment I had been shot at, and she couldn't contain her tears. Now she had found her son, and it didn't matter she and her daughters were as refugees.

As I approached, I could see her sorrow and pain fading away. Her tears turned into tears of joy, and she couldn't stop hugging me and thanking God for bringing me to her safely. We were happy to be alive, but we had to look for new way of living. Once again, we were back to zero. We had absolutely nothing to lean on. Only the grace of God sustained us.

Once again, I had escaped death. When I was going down, I said, "This is it." I didn't think I was going to make it out alive. I heard projectiles flying in all directions, and my new friend said, "Don't get up—just crawl."

I don't remember calling upon God—other than asking for forgiveness—but that was okay because He already knew I was in desperate need. He covered me under His mighty hand. That was why I could hear the bullets flying left and right and not harming me. I could see the corn shoots being cut in half, but I was protected.

I got up for a moment, and my friend shouted, "Don't get up—just crawl."

I tried to follow him, but it was impossible to keep

up with him. He must have been a soldier or had some kind of training, but I was just a simple teenager who had no idea what was going on—or why they were trying to kill us.

In the midst of it all, I could see the hand of God protecting me. Even with a stranger to help me to save myself, there was zero chance of survival. The promise of God is true when He says that He sends His angels to protect those He loves. His grace was more than just protecting me. He went beyond the limits of the righteous and saved seven more men. The unbelievers couldn't believe it was possible that they didn't get hit. I did not even have a scratch on me. The only thing I lost was my cowboy hat. One of the soldiers picked it up from the site and was parading it in front of my family. My family couldn't say anything for fear of implicating me.

I didn't understand what was going on, but I knew God was in control of my life. In order to show me His mighty hand, He had to put me through the fire. That way, I could see who my protector was. After seeing so much death and violence, I thought my chance of surviving the war was almost zero. Nevertheless, no matter where I went, there was not a single problem for me. There were checkpoints at almost at every main road near the major cities and towns, but I was never detained or questioned. I always saw how the hand of God was protecting me everywhere I went.

Others who had all their documents in order were

harassed, mistreated, or detained. Most of the time, they never returned to their families. Instead, the families had to go to the city morgues to find them. When they found them, they pretended they didn't know them. They didn't want to be next.

Although times were bad, God surrounded me with His protection. Even when I thought He had abandoned me, He never did. He always kept me safe under His mighty wings.

CHAPTER 11

A Refugee in My Own Country

To look into the past is not difficult, but knowing what lies ahead of you makes you uneasy. What did we do to deserve this? When will this stop? These are perhaps genuine questions that we ask when we are going through difficult moments. We think suffering should be off the list when it comes to us. Suffering is for someone else and never for us. I never questioned God directly when I found myself among people I didn't know. There were moments when I felt no different from them. The people who had been forsaken in those villages had no hope, and when I looked at them, I felt hopeless like them. I couldn't do anything to change their situation, but they were giving me from the little they had.

I never thought I was going to be a refugee in my own country. I really hated when people called me a refugee. It was so demeaning. I sometimes hid from people and wondered when it would be over. The night I spent among those villagers showed me so much, and I believe it was all the plan of God. I learned some valuable lessons. Those people had nothing, but their strong will seemed unbreakable. They didn't hesitate to shelter me and make sure I had at least a piece of blanket to cover myself.

They were on their last pound of rice, and a large number of people, including children, still needed to be fed. There was enough to feed me that day. They picked a man from among themselves who was brave enough to go to town to buy some groceries. I felt so bad that I couldn't cooperate with them, but I was broke. I didn't even have a cent to help them out. Suppertime came, and an old lady who had met me for the first time was treating me like family. She brought me a big portion of rice and beans and a few warm *tortillas*. I felt bad for taking these poor people's food, but I was starving and couldn't say no. When night rolled in, they asked if I wanted to stay on watch for a couple of hours. They gave me instructions in case the army showed up that night—something I didn't want to hear—but we had to be on the lookout.

Around nine o'clock, I was called in to go to sleep. One of the men said, "Come. This is the only spot available." He showed me a spot under a bed and handed me a piece of blanket. I didn't know if I should put it on the dirt floor or use it to cover myself. That was my breaking point, and I couldn't make any noise to pray or talk to anyone. My only choice was to stay quiet and listen to the Lord. I was more concerned with how I was going to get out of that forgotten place. I didn't want to be part of whatever was coming next.

I knew the army would not rest until they had killed the last villager. I had to get out of there before sunrise. Before they let me go, they had to make sure I was not going to reveal their hiding place. They asked if I was part of any organized antigovernment group. Saying no was going to raise suspicions, and then I would be in trouble. I hadn't shared my faith, and it seemed like they wanted to know who I was. I was afraid for a moment and wondered how I could convince them that I wasn't a threat. I said, "I am a Christian." I felt the power of God all over me, and everything went quiet.

Somewhere I heard someone saying, "He's okay then."

In my understanding, they didn't know what a Christian was or what I meant when I said I was a Christian.

There were no records that indicated that there was any Evangelical community. I'm not sure if they understood what I said to them. All I know is that when they heard me, it was like they had heard someone really important talking. The atmosphere changed, and they began treating me even more nicely and trying to help me find my way back to my family.

I knew the Spirit of God was there with me and within me, and God was going to bless those people. The scriptures say that even giving a glass of cold water to one of His little ones shall be rewarded—and even more for those poor people who gave more than a cup of water. The Lord made His way into that place, and I'm sure He brought me to those people. I believe God had those people in mind and was going to communicate His love to them and alleviate their suffering. He doesn't delight in any injustice.

I was ready to say goodbye and thank them for letting me be part of their group for a night. The night was filled with terror. All I could hear were weird noises like owls and other scavengers that were roaming around just blocks away. The dogs that were left behind cried all night. It was unbearable to hear the poor animals that had been abandoned with no humans to take care of them. In most cases, the owners had been killed. Others simply couldn't take care of them since they had lost everything.

I was glad the night was over and that I was on my way to find my mother and the rest of my family. They provided a guide who got me to the main road safely. My journey was supposed to last four hours, but I made it home in about three. I ran as much as I could and tried to get to my mother and sisters as soon as I could. When I got home, my mother and sisters were gone.

My big sister and I talked for a few minutes, and then I was back on the road. I had no clue that my mother, my two other sisters, and other kids were hiding in a refugee camp. When I got there, all these people from my village were hiding from the army. They thought they were going to be safe at *the finca de Don Pedro*. It was a huge place surrounded with corridors and tile floors, but the corridors were full of refugees who had invaded the place—whether it was okay with *Don Pedro* or not. He was a nice man who sheltered all those people without any complaints. He tried to help all of them and fed them while they were there.

My mother couldn't travel back to our village that day. We decided to wait another day to give her time to recuperate. The next morning, my mother still wasn't ready to journey home. We decided one of my sisters and her kids could travel back. Since I had made my way there, I knew it was okay for them to make their way back. My sister and her kids went home to get things ready. The plan was to leave the village if we wanted to spare our lives.

On the third day, my mother still wasn't feeling well enough to take the road home. The worst of all was that when they got there, they had only asked to spend the night. We didn't want to abuse *Don Pedro*'s goodwill. Most of the people had left, and it was almost just the three of us. My mom and little sister were sleeping in the open corridor. The only good thing was that we were under a roof, but it wasn't fun waking up on the morning and seeing some of *Don Pedro*'s neighbors looking at us like we were from another planet. That went on for a week, and I was not okay with it. To make things worse, there was a neighbor named Mary. She was the same age as me, and she used to get up before me and rush to where we were sleeping to talk to me. She was trying to be nice. It was not that I didn't like it, but it was embarrassing to let her see me sleeping on that floor. She invited me to meet her parents and have coffee with them. At least that made me forget the situation for a moment. They were nice people who cared for others.

By the end of the week, we were the last ones there. My big sister was worried that we were not coming, and she decided to find out for herself what was happening to us. Although she was a city girl and wasn't used to long walks in the middle of nowhere, she trusted one of the kids who had returned from that refugee site to lead her there. It took them four hours, but she hadn't seen my mother since the day of the shooting. Since there was no other way to communicate, she had no choice but to go herself.

As soon as she arrived, I introduced her to Mary. They became good friends and didn't want to let us go. We ended up staying for a few more days.

My mother had become friends with some of the ladies at the *finca de Don Pedro*, but it was time to say goodbye. I had to say goodbye to my friend who was there for me during that time, and I didn't know how to tell her that it was a forever goodbye. It wasn't in my plans to return there again. Our decision had been made to move to the opposite corner of the country. There was not a chance that I would return to that place because the circumstances we lived in made it impossible.

If Mary asked if I was going back to see her, I didn't

know how I was going to say, "I won't see you again." It isn't in my heart to use people, and I knew we owed them and had to show them our gratitude somehow. My sister managed to smooth things out with the possibility that we were going to be back at some point. Finally, we got together at Mary's house and hugged after we thanked them for all they had done for us. That was the last time we saw those wonderful people God put in our way to help us. Even when we thought we had nothing left and nowhere to go, God surprised us by putting people of goodwill on our path.

After we said goodbye to everyone, we took that road back to our house. My mother still wasn't feeling well. She was not in a condition to travel such a long distance on foot, but we had no choice. It took almost the whole day to make it back to our village. She had trouble with the idea that we were moving out of the village where we thought we had finally made our home. It never crossed our minds that we were going to be homeless again that year. It was hard to leave everything we had acquired in our new place, but we had no choice. It had been a warning, and we were not going to take a chance and stay any longer, and we were glad we didn't. After we left the place we had called home for a year, the forces of evil broke loose. Some of the villagers organized themselves in what they called *Defensa Civil*, but it was more like a group of armed criminals. They slaughtered their own people, but we were far gone by then. Thank God!

It didn't take us long to gather all our belongings, and we didn't have much to carry. In a couple days, we were out of that place. We were going back in the direction we had come from, but we were going to try the city for a change. We moved only on the expectation that people and relatives were going to be compassionate enough to open their doors to us.

My big sister didn't rest until she got us out of there. Her plans didn't turn out exactly the way she hoped, but we found an uncle who was able to take us into his house temporarily. He gave us a room that was able to accommodate all seven of us. The tenants at Grandpa's house didn't have a clue we were coming, but one of my uncles was in charge of the property. He found a way to evict them, and we move in after two months. Our challenge was making a living in a new place. We found a good church, and we got connected right away. They helped me find work.

It wasn't in my book to be a refugee in my own country. Bouncing from place to place didn't give me any pleasure, but in the midst of all of that, God was molding my character. If I knew what was waiting for me, I never would have thought I would make it through. I was walking through a dark tunnel, and my only hope was Jesus. He had told me on many occasions not to worry. He said, "I will be with you even in the darkest days of your life." That hope helped me to carry on into the unknown.

Although there were days when I didn't see how

that was going to be possible, a little voice inside of me kept saying, "Don't be afraid. You'll see tomorrow." I learned to trust in the Lord and listen to His voice. My relationship with the Lord grew bigger and bigger, and I was being given an opportunity to experience His power firsthand. Not everyone gets to walk really close to the edge of death and make it unharmed. Even when I was at the refugee sites and feeling no more special than the rest of the people who didn't know the Lord, I was being watched over. I didn't even know it. Even when I didn't fully understand that mercy and grace were following me everywhere I went, I was able to see the difference around me. A precious experience brought me closer to the Lord, and that experience caused me a great deal of suffering. In the end, I learned that I hadn't been walking alone.

CHAPTER 12

My Business Partner and His Disappearance

Is it true that there is peace after every storm? Sometimes it looks like the storm never ends. If it does, we most likely have been caught in the middle.

I might have lost everything, but the one thing I never lost was hope. I was always looking for ways to improve my living conditions and support my mother. I was the one staying with her, and that gave me a sense of responsibility. I felt like I had to set the mark to where our family would go. I was on a mission to make things better. Although I had left the place of my birth and spent a year somewhere else, I felt like my home was wherever I went. Even when I was building toward my future and seeing people trying to destroy everything I had built—I never stop trying. I remember when I was a kid, my brother used to break everything I had proudly built—but that never stopped me from pursuing my goals. If it got destroyed, I used to built it again.

A few weeks had gone by, and work was scarce. I was working a few days here and there, and I was trying to reconfigure my strategy to see how I could survive in an environment I wasn't used to. I am thankful for the people God put in my way to help me find work in an environment I didn't know, but people were constantly being killed in army clashes. It was normal to get up in the morning and find dead people all over. Sometimes there were clashes during working hours, and people just ducked under the bullets. Minutes later, they were back to business after the fire department and ambulances had cleaned the mess. That was the environment I was moving into. That lifestyle was normal for others—but not for me. People were going to sleep at night, but they didn't know if they were going to end up dead in a ditch in the morning. Those amazing people were determined to make it regardless of the situation they were living in. Such attitudes inspired me to do something different. I began by signing up for night school. I needed time during the day to work and provide for myself and my mother.

Although it wasn't easy to start anything and make it work, I had to come up with an idea and make it work if I wanted to survive in the city. I didn't have any other place else to go. I was there, and I had to find something that would give me a steady income.

I continued working and hoped to put a plan in action as soon as possible. I was taking any work I could find as bricklayer's assistant and going to school and church. I had found a way to stay busy, but I was lacking a position of employment or a place where I would say, "This is what I will be doing for a long term."

I was getting used to the bombs and shootings that were leaving so many dead. To give comfort in that time, people said, "Tomorrow will be a better day. Therefore, we won't stop dreaming about good future." For many people, those dreams never came through. Their lives were taken before they had a chance to see the future they were dreaming of.

There was hope for those who couldn't leave the country. They hoped things would get better. We said, "There isn't an illness that will last for a hundred years—or a patient who can take it for that long." We all hoped the end of the war was near. For four years, we had endured more than enough. We thought we had seen it all by then, but we didn't know that there were another eight years left in that brutal war.

After a few months, I still had no idea what I was going to do—and then I ran into Theodore. He knew someone who knew how to start a business. Theodore was a good man who had run away from his village in search of better life for his seven kids and his wife. Like many of us, he left his livelihood behind. He had to abandon his land and his house to protect his family from being bombed or killed in the rural area where he lived. His big task was supporting his large family, but that didn't bother him because he feared nothing. He told me he was going to see a friend and find out more about the kind of business he was in.

An hour later, Theodore came back and told me he was going for training with his friend the next day. He said, "I will go and learn everything we need, and then we will go in partnership with this."

That sounded great to me—even though I had no idea what exactly or where I was going to get the money to finance it. That was what I liked about Theodore. He never saw limits, and he always thought wherever there was a will, there was a way. He spent a week training with his friend and getting all the connections needed for us to begin the process. The business wasn't complicated. It wasn't more than hard labor and finding a clientele. The three major components of the business were money, clientele, and a good location for the base of operations.

The business consisted of dehydrating limestone or "burning limestone." The rocks were mined and sold as raw limestone. Industries burn them by adding water to activate the chemicals within the rocks, heating them up to the point of melting and releasing all gases. This process creates a pure white fine powder that is widely used for many things throughout Central and South America. The mineral is rich in calcium, magnesium, and other minerals that are good for the human body. These days, it is mostly used to boil corn to make it easier to clean. We were told it provides the calcium needed for teeth and bones. The corn was processed for the preparation of *tortillas*. It is still used in almost every home in many countries. We knew there was a big market for it, and we had to act fast.

I was living at my grandpa's house, and there was also a small house that he had built in the back yard for one of his daughters. My aunts had gone to one of the neighboring countries with Grandpa. The little house was about four hundred square feet, and it was the perfect base for our new business. I had the place to set our new business, and all we needed was the other two components to make our dream a reality.

Perhaps the money wouldn't be that difficult since there was the possibility of starting small to see if it would work. The real challenge was building a clientele in a city of thirty or forty thousand people. Selling our product door-to-door wasn't an option. Taking that route would force us and our families into starvation, and that is when I went back to what I knew best.

I asked the Lord for help, but I didn't hear anything in a supernatural way. I bought a beautiful painting, and I decided it would look good right above my front door, which was facing a busy street. As crazy is it sounds, I knew God had promised to be with me. Moreover, even if I found myself in the middle of a desert, the mighty hand of God was going to lead me through.

I framed and nailed that beautiful fourteen-by-sixteen

picture above my front door, but it wasn't advertising the name of my business. Instead, it was declaring that whatever I was about to do was going to be prosperous. My desire was to let everybody who traveled through that avenue see that picture. The message written on that picture was Psalm 1, but what affected me most was the last part of verse 3.

I had a deep conviction that God's blessing would follow me. Therefore, everything I intended to do would make it grow. I thought my only choice was to trust God since there was no business plan to follow or any other business model I could rely on. I only knew I had to come up with something fast because there was no time to waste. Every day that went by was a challenge to make it in a place where everything from a lemon to meat needed to be bought. It wasn't like that where I was from. I was used to just going to the fields and picking whatever I wanted to eat—from a mango to a sweet pineapple. Everything I wanted to eat was there, and now I was in a place where I had to have the cash on hand if I wanted something. I wasn't used to that different lifestyle, but I knew I was not alone.

I discussed the logistics of the business with Theodore, and the only solution we came up with was going to all the stores in that city to show them our product. There was no way to advertise other than radio and newspaper, and that would be very expensive. Secondly, the nature of our product didn't qualify for that. The product was too basic to go in that direction, but we needed to get it into the market—and it had to be me who had to pushed it through. We figured that part out, but we hadn't talked to other businesses about what we were planning. Our plan was to create a few samples and show our product to store owners. We needed to come up with the capital to lift it off the ground, and that was going to be hard since no bank would lend us money. Banks didn't know us, and we had no collateral or valuables. I was just turning seventeen, and what financial institution would trust me and give me a loan?

We came up with a little bit of money. It was enough to buy a few pounds of the raw material and the wrappings so we could make one sample. After we got the starting money, one of the kids and I went to a store and bought twenty-five pounds of raw limestone. Our mission was to determine who their supplier was so we could get the material straight from the source—or from the mining company since our vision was so big.

Right after we got home with the supplies, Theodore and I went into that little house and began the dehydration process. We were excited because we wanted to see how the final product was going to turn out. I was ready to make some sales. We were so happy to see how a big solid rock could discharge its gases and turn into a white crystalline powder. We watched the birth of what we believed was going to be the beginning of our company. Our company would generate enough income for both of us, and it would generate employment for some of our neighbors. We left the material in the corner, closed the doors behind us, and hoped to start the work in the morning. Our dream was turning into reality.

We didn't have any idea how we were going to finance the operation, but we were going forward with our plans. Everything was going according to plan, but we had not stopped to think about where the funds would come from. We only knew that we wanted it to happen, and somehow, we knew we were going to make it. Theodore's attitude was always positive. We were going to have whatever money we needed to get this thing in full swing.

At times, I thought he was delusional because of the way he talked. It didn't make any sense to me. He was trying to do something from noting, but I understood that God had placed him around me so I could see what was possible for those who trust in Him. I was the believer, but sometimes I couldn't grasp what God had intended to do before my eyes. I understood that God had many ways to accomplish His purposes in me.

God used Theodore to show me how He was going to deliver me from economic hardship. In my mind, none of what we were doing made any sense. It was impossible to think a few rocks would help me sustain myself, provide for my mother, and bring my tithes and offerings to my church. Perhaps my teenage brain was not able to comprehend the magnitude of my God, but I realize it wasn't me who was sustaining myself. It was Him—the great I Am—who had not let me go. He was the one who had me in His hand—regardless of my weaknesses and failures.

Even though Theodore wasn't aware of the reason why he was there, he served a purpose for God. The time we spent working was the great opportunity God had designed for him. When we get a chance to look back, we realize that our journey wouldn't have been possible if something or someone greater had not made it possible. In this case, as much as it was for me or for Theodore, the power of God was manifested in the midst of adversity.

In the morning, we went to our shop, which was going to be our factory, to see what had happened with what we had left there. To our surprise, our very first batch had come out just the way we had hoped. We had done everything right, and now we had the recipe to carry on. It was time to get to work on our first sample.

I was excited and worried. How was I going to promote the product if I had no training or experience as a salesman? I had to figure out how I was going to walk into a store, ask for the manager, and try to convince that person that I had in my possession the product they had been waiting for. Theodore had no doubts that I was capable of doing it, and he never wasted any time trying to help me get ready for my presentation. Instead, he bagged the product so I could begin my journey as a salesman. He was going to stay behind and make sure we could fill the upcoming orders. We only had enough material to produce a bit more than the samples we had decided to prepare. If I sold a big order, I had no clue how we could produce it. Our second plan wasn't fully developed, but we were ready to go. Before I knew it, my first sample was ready to go. It was all about making my first sale. Nervously, I began to get ready. I looked for my best clothes and my best pair of shoes. I was going to make the journey on foot, but I had to be presentable.

It was about ten o'clock when we finished the first sample, and I only had two hours before lunch. As usual, the stores closed for two hours at lunchtime and reopened at two. They stayed open until five at the latest. If I were to miss the morning hours, I would have to wait for the following day to show my product. I ran to a store that was on my way to downtown.

I had a feeling I was going to go into that store—and I wasn't coming out of there empty-handed. I ran into someone from my youth group at church, and I asked him to give me a ride on his bicycle. He agreed to take me there to try to sell my product. I wanted to try that store because the people there were in the wholesale business. I knew they were supplying other businesses, and I had a good chance of making a big sale there.

I didn't know the store owner, but I had met one of the sons at church. Unfortunately, he wasn't there—only his mother but she was the right person to talk to. I still have no idea how I introduced myself, but whatever I did seemed to work.

At the end of my presentation, she said, "I want three hundred bags."

"Three hundred? No problem. You'll have them by tomorrow." I walked out of that place like I was walking on the clouds. I had just made a sale close to three hundred *colones*, which was more than a month's salary for a regular worker. I knew we did not have enough supply to produce that quantity of bags for the following day, but we had to come up with the money that day to buy the rest of the supply and get it ready. Each bag contained sixty packages of approximately three ounces each. Three hundred bags was going to be a big job. Fortunately, we had people ready for packaging. What we didn't have was the money we needed.

I ran as fast as I could to get the news to Theodore and my mother. Theodore told me to give him a few minutes. He was going to get some money, and we could go get the rest of the supplies to finish the order.

Soon enough, Theodore came back with enough money to get what we needed for the first big order. We began the process and worked on the logistics of the business. We had yet to contact the mining company at the other end of the country and find out what we needed—other than money—for them to make a delivery. We had managed to get their direct contact and cut out the middleman's cost. Fortunately, they only need a thousand *colones* for a deposit. That was almost the equivalent of one year of wages for an average person, and we didn't have that kind of money in our possession.

We looked at each other and said, "What do we do now?" We had hit a dead end.

It was almost impossible for us to get a thousand *colones*—and then I thought of my big sister. She could probably help us. I knew that it was going to be a bit hard to explain my business plan over the phone and convince her that it was okay to lend me money for something she didn't fully understand.

I went to find a pay phone, and it didn't take long to convince her after I explained my business plan. "Better yet," I said, "we already sold a big order."

That was enough for her to tell me that she was on board. "I will be taking the first bus tomorrow to see you," she said. It was going to take her almost a full day, but I was going to get her to see what I was talking about. I ran home to share the good news to Theodore. "My big sister is coming. She is going to come up with a solution to our problem."

At the shop, the production was in progress. Even though the logistics of the business weren't complete, I had to carry on with my sales.

The following day, we all were excited that my sister was coming to what we now called home. We had not seen her since the last horrible incident a few months back. It was so dangerous to travel in those days. Everybody was afraid to step on the streets without fearing an explosion or clashes between the rebels and the army. Everybody was afraid to go out of their houses and not come back. My big sister knew better since she had experienced it herself.

She arrived the next day, and we all were happy to see her again. We were in our third home, which she had originally worked to get us into. It was a great reunion after all we had gone through. It was more like a dream. After just a few months, we were in a totally different position. We were in good health, and we were doing something good with our lives.

We had lined up people to work in our factory. A few single mothers and some young people who were good to work after school, which gave them an opportunity to earn money for school supplies. The whole plan looked great, and we had already started it. The only thing missing was the funds to make it bigger.

When my big sister saw all that we had done, she thought it was a good idea and a good investment in that community. She took me to one of the five banks in the city to open an account. I had no clue what she was planning to do. I only knew that I was with my big sister and that I was going to get the money to carry on with what I had started. She made me dress in my best clothes and clean my only pair of shoes so I could walk into that bank as an important businessman.

For the first time in my life, I was treated with respect. Someone even opened the door for me. I still didn't know what she was planning on doing. I wasn't sure whether she was going to try to get us a loan or borrow it herself to pass it on to my account.

When one of the bank officials approached us, my sister said that I was there to open an account because I was starting a business and was going to be depositing some money.

I was astounded. I had no money. *What is she talking about?*

The bank official said, "Very well then" and began writing down all my information.

I never questioned what my sister was doing. I was fully confident that she knew what she was doing, and I just followed her instructions.

When the bank lady asked how much I was going to open my account with, I went mute and waited for my sister to answer.

The lady looked her, and my big sister said, "He will open it with one thousand *colones*."

A thousand colones at my disposal? I thought.

My big sister opened her purse, pulled out the money, and handed it to me with no return address. I knew she was a hard saver, but I never imagined she would simply hand me that kind of money and walk away.

We wrapped up with all we needed to do there, and I walked out of that bank feeling rich. I only had the opportunity to see the money and left with just the bank book stating that I was a thousand *colones* richer. I had the funds to carry on with what I had started, but the mining company wanted those thousand colones as a deposit. We had to do something to get the company to deliver the product to our house.

Theodore thought we could convince them to make a delivery and pay cash upon arrival. I thought it was going to be hard to convince them because they had already told me I had to wire them the money first. It was obvious since they did not know who we were. When they heard a young kid on the phone, they probably thought it was a joke.

Theodore never gave up. He thought the company might send an eight-ton truck full of limestone to random people and hope to get paid. Finally, he convinced me.

I went back to the phone booth and called again. Although it wasn't that close, I had no choice but to walk five blocks to get to the phone. By the time I got there, it was too late. The office was closed for the day. I had to go back the next morning and call them again—and make sure I didn't return without good news.

The following morning, I went to the pay phone and made the call.

The secretary asked how to direct my call.

Since I did not know who I should talk to, I asked her to put me through to the shipping department.

The person in charge asked me my account name, but I didn't have one.

I told him I wanted to open an account and get them to deliver a big order of limestone.

"Well, that is possible, but before we send you the product, we will need a deposit."

I said, "I don't have time to waste. Please send me the product, and I will pay you in cash as soon your men unload the product at my storage."

The man replied, "We can't send our trucks all the way there for less than four tons."

I said, "No worries. Send me five tons, and I'll have your money ready."

The man agreed to send five tons without any money down—relying only on my word that I was going to have his money upon receiving the product. I had convinced the man to send a crew of three men, and they had to drive six or seven hours to reach my destination. I was amazed. According to their protocol, that wasn't supposed to happen. Something had happened to make this man trust a seventeen-year-old with the value of almost a thousand colones.

I ran home to share the news with Theodore and my mom. I expected them to say, "I told you so."

Instead, I was encouraged to move to the next step, which it was to go see some other businesses and offer them the product. The shipment was supposed to take three days to get to our place, and we were confident that we were not going to be undersold. The pressure was on me. I had to sell more than what I had sold before.

I began to visit new places, but not many were interested in my product. It was kind of discouraging. We had all that material coming to us, and we had the money—but what we were going to do with five tons of limestone if I didn't sell anything? I only had one customer, and I needed at least fifty of those customers to survive. I managed to sell a few bags here and there while we were getting ready for the big shipment to arrive.

Theodore never gave up, and he was always enthusiastic about it. He thought we were going to be successful. He thought our new business was going to be a machine carving into the future and providing us what we needed to survive. Perhaps because he wasn't the one trying to make a sale, he had no idea what I was going through. Nevertheless, his attitude was an important ingredient in the business. At times, he could see the details that I couldn't. I was still learning about life, and he had been around much longer. He was able to see thing differently, and that was the combination that was needed to make things work.

The eight-ton truck carrying the first load of limestone rocks parked right in front of the house and was ready to be unloaded. What days before was just a dream was now right in front of our eyes. I was excited to see the men unloading that enormous load. I knew they were going to take a while since they had to do it all by hand.

The driver said, "I hope you have the money ready."

I said, "Continue with your job, and before you finish,

I'll be back from the bank with your money." I went to the bank to withdraw the money to pay for the product we had ordered. I had told the company we were going to require that same quantity at least once a month. I had faith that I was somehow going to get into the market. I was confident that my product was far superior to everyone else's, and that was going to give me an advantage over those producers. There were many others who had their limestone product on the market before us, but I believed I could do better than those people. I believed that everything I began would prosper. I was there because God had brought me there. He planned to show me what he was capable of doing for me. He wasn't done with me yet. He had raised me up higher than what I had envisioned. It wasn't normal for a sixteen-year-old who had lost everything, including his father, to be looked at with the kind of respect I was being looked at with. He had poured His grace upon me, and I wasn't even aware of it. I had found that people had no trouble trusting me—even when I had no material things to back me up. Business people were not afraid to deal with me. They didn't think I was too young to make any kind of deal.

The bank was about an hour away by bus, and the people were about finished unloading the product when I came back with their money. The transaction went smoothly. I counted out the money, and they signed the contract. I had to report to the office that I had received the product in full. I had to find a way to sell five tons of dehydrated-limestone before the month was over.

We set up a batch to cook overnight so it would be ready for packaging in the morning. We had already lined up the people for the packaging, and they were to be paid daily for every piece. We had missed one detail though. None of us had discussed where we were going to get the money to pay our employees. We had not planned that part since our main focus was on raising our inventory to be ready for the big incoming orders. We refused to think we were going to stay small. We were building a company with the capacity to supply distributers that were going to move our product throughout the country, yet we had forgotten to allocate the funds that would cover the workers.

I had some money left in the bank—plus the money I had made from a few sales here and there—but that wouldn't be enough if I didn't sell anything for the first few weeks. What were we going to do? What was our plan B?

The pressure was building, and I took the samples to more wholesale stores and offered my product, hoping to make the sale of the month. It didn't go so well. I just managed to make a few small sales, and I had to go back to my original client to see how she was doing. To my surprise, she placed another order that was bigger than her first one. That raised my hopes, but I needed more customers like her. That day, I returned home not completely empty-handed. At least we had some money coming in to help us move forward. Although there were no dividends yet, we had to continue pressing on until we could find the right costumers who would buy our product in large quantities.

Days and weeks went by, and we were still waiting for the breakthrough we desperately needed. I usually went to church every day, except Mondays, after I finished working. I would walk to church along with my mom. On weekends, I was more involved. Saturday was youth day, and I was always preaching or serving in other areas that day. That helped me create a network of friends, and from time to time, they would give me business leads.

Theodore was given a lead about a potential buyer. The lead was kind of vague, and Theodore had only been told that the man had a small store nearby. Since we were in a tight situation, I had to find him—even if I had to check all the stores near me.

The following day, I got up early, grabbed my samples, and took along one of the kids. We had to go through all the stores in the area—big and small.

Close to noon, we got to a very small store that was facing to the street. The kid and I were skeptical of the place, but I found the courage to ask to speak with the owner.

A lady came out and asked what we wanted—and if there was anything she could help us with.

I introduced myself as the representative of the

company that was producing the best dehydrated limestone and was capable of delivering any quantity at any time. I said, "I have some samples for you to look at."

She asked to look at them, and after checking them out, she said, "Come back at two o'clock. My husband will be here."

"That can be arranged," I replied.

We believed we had gone to the right place with our product. It took us about an hour to walk home, have lunch, and walk back to see the man.

At two o'clock, we were waiting for them to open. We didn't want to leave anything to chance, and we had to try our best to make a sale. We had no idea what was beyond the storefront, and we needed to find out what kind of business it was. We were not to leave a stone unturned until we found out what was hiding behind those walls. There was a big industrial garage door and a big driveway, but beyond that, nothing would suggest there was more to it.

We waited outside for about ten minutes, and then I knocked on the door.

The lady opened the door and asked us to give them a few minutes since they were still having lunch.

A man called to her to let me in, and she walked me through the store to the back.

A shirtless man was eating his meal at a huge dining table. He said, "What do you have for me?"

"The best product money can buy," I said.

He asked to have a look, and I showed it to him. He said, "All right. I like it. I will pay you six hundred *colones* for every thousand bags. Bring me as much as you can produce."

"All right," I said. I didn't have to negotiate the price since I knew he was right on with it. "I will be here tomorrow with the first load."

We were stunned. A thousand bags was a huge load since each bag contained sixty packages of approximately three ounces each. To produce that quantity wasn't easy, but we already had the people working like we knew something big was coming. If the man followed through on his word, we wouldn't have to struggle to find more clients. If we could produce a thousand bags per week with the people we had working, it was going to be good enough for us. It was going to give us approximately four months of salary for an average person in a week.

When I got home, Theodore was waiting to hear about our visit with the new client. I couldn't contain my excitement. I had good news written all over my face, but he wasn't able to determine how good the news was. It was going to put us in front of all the other producers in the region. We would even be ahead of the warehouse that had been in business for years. The other producers were buying from the warehouse because it was the only available place in the city. We had to buy there the first couple of times, and that was where we got the connection to buy straight from the mining company. Our first order was larger than what the local store used to buy, and our buying power was automatically greater. It was the breakthrough we were waiting for. We found a way to get rid of the mountain of raw limestone we had purchased, and the company delivered the second load just as promised. I had to keep buying at least once a month to keep the account open. That channel was going to triple our profit, and give us the flexibility to compete in the market.

I shared the good news with Theodore, and he was just excited as I was. We didn't have a written contract, but we trusted the verbal agreement and handshake. That was how we used to make deals, and we were not afraid of the man bluffing or doing something funny.

We worked hard to deliver the first big order and finished around noon the following day. I rushed downtown to where the truck and pickup owners offered transportation services. I had to start my delivery by three o'clock. I wasn't missing the opportunity, and I pushed everybody to accomplish our goal. I wanted to see the money all at once since it was going to be close to what we had invested in the first load. From then on, we were going to start seeing money for ourselves. We were into the second month, and we had seen no profits.

The moment of truth had come, and we were ready to ship out the biggest order we had produced. A thousand bags were loaded onto a truck and were ready to be delivered to our new customer. As I was going there, negative thoughts creeped into my mind. *What if this man closes the door on me and says he's never seen me? What will I do with all of this product?*

I realized that faith is calling things that haven't yet been seen. I had to keep moving forward until I got to the man's house to see for myself what he was hiding behind the walls at the back of the store. I was curious about what was beyond the big dining table. I had to show the guys with me that I was in charge of the situation—and that everything was going to be all right.

It only took fifteen minutes to get to our destination. I walked into the store and felt stronger than the first time. I greeted the people and let them know I had a truck outside with their first order of one thousand bags of pure, clean translucent limestone—just the way they wanted.

The man wasn't home, but he had left his wife in charge of receiving the order.

She didn't seem impressed with the quantity. She just told an employee to let us in. After he opened the huge garage door, we drove into the warehouse. I was finally going to satisfy my curiosity. I wondered what gave the man such great buying power if what I had seen wasn't more than a few things that probably wouldn't earn a hundred *colones* per day. How did he have the power to buy his merchandise in a large quantities? Was the man's business genuine or not? I was not convinced by the way he had conducted his business with me. I was not even sure he was going to buy from me.

I had finally gotten to the point where I wanted to be. Inside the warehouse, I saw the proof I had wanted to see. At the back of the store, there were many rooms filled with all kinds of products. It looked like he supplied many stores across the country.

The employee took me to an empty room and said, "This is where you will be storing your product."

I was excited and went back to the truck. "Now you know where to unload your truck"

"What? No one will be checking on us to make sure we drop the product in full?"

I said myself, "I guess not."

They asked what I had seen in there.

"No worries. There is a plenty of room for our product," I said. "Follow me"

We began to unload the truck, hoping to come out of there six hundred *colones* richer.

When we finished unloading, I made my way to the counter to collect my payment.

The lady asked if I had dropped all the product.

I told her I had unloaded one thousand bags, and that was enough for her to hand me the payment in full. She had trusted me, and there was no need to send someone back there to check whether I had dropped the product I was trying to collect payment for.

She handed in the money, and I told her I would be back before the weekend.

She said that it was okay, and I told my guys to hurry

because we had to bring another load before the end of the week. I knew it was kind of ambitious, but I wanted to push it hard and produce two thousand bags per week. That would give us twelve hundred *colones* per week, which was an amazing financial breakthrough for us.

It was great news for Theodore too. He was waiting for me to count the money, and he liked the idea of pumping up production. We could deliver two big orders in a week. He thought it wouldn't be a problem, and he began moving things around. He said, "You'll have your order ready by Friday." It was Wednesday afternoon, but for him, nothing seemed too difficult. We all worked hard that week to accomplish what we wanted. Before we knew it, we had managed to bag the next order. That one was much easier since we knew the way.

I proceeded the same way, but I was more confident that we were on the right track. When I got there, all I had to do was notify them that I was coming in with a load. They only had to let me in since I knew where I needed to go.

The operation went smoothly, which was what I was looking for. I had been able to collect the money without any trouble, which made me happy, and we had made our product known beyond our city. We had found the right channel to bring it to thousands of homes, and many were using our product. We were going to soar above and beyond. There was no going back on our business plan. Everything was going according to what we had envisioned.

For months, we had managed to keep things on schedule. Money was no problem, and Theodore managed to save enough to buy his own house. Since he had no difficulty making things work, he closed a deal on a house. It wasn't a big house, but it was a great start for his family. He only needed a day to close the deal on his house. I was surprised to hear he had accomplished so much in so little time, but I was happy for him. It inspired me to keep pushing hard and reap the benefits of my hard labor. From there, it was a matter of concentrating on what we had established and getting more people to increase our production. We employed a few more people, and we were happy to help more single mothers. Our dream was benefiting others who were in desperate situations.

The past had no impact on our lives anymore. My mother was doing very well, my little sister was doing well in school, and I was involved more than ever at church. All my worries had been taken away, and I was enjoying life the way it was meant for me. I was in a position that not just anyone could rise to in nine months. I had arrived that city with just the clothes on my back, hoping to find refuge for me and family members.

My other sisters were also doing well. One of them had started her own baking business to support her children. My other sister had hardly made herself visible, and another brother had left the country before the war. We were happy to not be haunted by our past.

I continued working hard. I had finally found an occupation to provide for my mom and for myself. I was always thankful to the Lord for giving me all the people who surrounded me. I had everything I needed, but I was not to let my guard down. We were still living in war times. I had seen God getting water from the rock for my sake. He had promised that He was not leaving me, but it was necessary to put me through the fire from time to time. When it all seemed to be going right, He would put me through another test to see how much I believed Him. I was not focused on what I could do. I focused in Him instead.

The business was flourishing, and I was able to take care of all my needs and help my mother. I wasn't worried about what was going to happen down the road. I felt spiritual and physical protection. I was enjoying the peace God had promised me when I was saved. It was a new beginning for me. I learned new things and made new friends. I was grateful for the people God had placed near me, and I learned a great deal. I spent my weekends in church with my church friends and serving in whatever ways I could. I felt like I had found my purpose in life. I never thought God brought me to a temporary oasis to gain strength because there was a long way to go.

Time went by, and everything was great. We were happy with our earnings and making plans to extend our business operations. After we finished the day's work, Theodore wrapped things up and went to be with his wife and children. I went to church and got back around eight, which was the latest we could be out. Our church services started at three so we could be back in our homes early. No one wanted to go out late at night; nighttime was the terror hours. We only risked stepping outside if there was a serious emergency.

Theodore always left extra time to travel back and forth to his house. He had to walk about half an hour to get to his new house and made sure there was still daylight during the walk. That day was different. As he was getting ready for work at five o'clock in the morning, he heard a knock at the door. Being an honest man and fearing nothing, he got up to see who could be knocking so early in the morning.

Three men aimed their rifles at him and brutally apprehended him without an explanation. That sent a shock wave through the house, awakening everybody— even the baby. When the men were surrounded by Theodore's family, they questioned him in a more humane manner. Everybody knew how the death squads operated, and Theodore's family knew he had been targeted.

When the men saw everybody crying and clinging to Theodore, they told his wife and kids that they were just taking him in for questioning. That gave Theodore and his family a small ray of hope. He thought he was going to see his loved ones again, and so did his wife and kids.

However, that wasn't the case. Once he was in the hands of those murderers, it was the point of no return.

They handcuffed him and put him in a vehicle with the promise that they were only bringing him in for questioning—but they never said where they were taking him. The normal thing to do would be to bring him to a police station for the investigation, but it never happened that way. They took him to the place where they took all political prisoners to torture them. The prisoners had no chance for a phone call to a lawyer or to their families— never mind having visitors. Once they were there, they were destined to be executed.

Theodore's wife didn't want to believe that was going to be his fate.

One of his kids ran to my house, and I was still in bed, thinking it was going to be another profitable day for us. I wasn't prepared to hear someone knocking at my door crying—never mind to hear that Theodore had been taken. I was scared when I heard someone crying at my front door, but I got up to check who it was.

As soon as I opened the door, Theodore's kid said, "They have taken him."

I wasn't fully awake yet. "Who have they taken?"

"My father."

I automatically knew what he was talking about. For us, it was only a matter of when they would come knocking at our doors. No one was safe, and we were never sure if we were going to see another day. That was the reality we lived every day, and there was nothing we could have done about it.

My mother and I got ready to go see the pastor and some other influential people from church. We were hoping to get some help to find out where were they holding Theodore. His wife was working around the clock to find him. She was relying on the promises of the men who had taken him. From my own experiences, I knew there was no chance for Theodore to make it back. As much as I wanted to be optimistic, I couldn't reconcile the idea that I was going to see Theodore again. We talked to someone at church who had an important relative in the army to see if he could help us to locate Theodore, but it was useless. His wife was trying everywhere, including the international entities that were there to help in such situations, but she was coming up with empty promises. We checked the morgues for his body but found nothing. The situation grew more uncertain by the day. There was a chance he was alive, and every time we heard of a body being found along the road, we went to make sure it wasn't Theodore.

That was the beginning of the collapse of our company. Within two weeks, I was forced to shut down the operations—for my own sake and my mother's sake. My mother thought I was going to disappear next, and she couldn't bear the idea of her son suffering the same fate as Theodore. I had no other choice but to leave everything behind and go look for my big sister. She was always able to reach out to me. It was hard to see all my accomplishments and dreams going down the drain, but I had no other way to protect myself.

I was sad to leave my church and my friends behind without an explanation. My decision to leave was swift. The danger had landed close enough. I had nothing to do with what was going on, and I felt like I was being persecuted. The only thing that was keeping me alive was the grace of God. I didn't understand why every time things were getting better for me, trouble would cause disruption and leave me dispossessed. I chose to trust God. He was walking me literal through the valley of death, and He was going to get me through.

Theodore's tragedy and other tragedies marked my path forever. I didn't understand the meaning of it all. How was it possible to lose everything in a moment? I had seen the hand of God working on my behalf—and then everything was gone forever, leaving only memories. We had started a business from nothing, and we had gotten to the point where we thought we had made it. We had survived hardship, and we had been able to provide for our families, but all our efforts were now gone.

Theodore had put all his efforts into the business since the day he approached me with the idea of becoming business partners. He had a vision that we were going to make it and be successful. His passion in pursuing his goals taught me to be diligent and persistent in order to obtain what I wanted. His disappearance was a loss to his family and to many of us who knew him. A senseless act took a father away from seven children and a wife, leaving them to the mercy of time. There was no one else to come to their aid. His wife was left with the responsibility of raising those kids. Theodore had sacrificed himself to give them a better life, and they were all alone—waiting for the only father they had known. They hoped he was going to return someday, and his wife wished it was just a nightmare. She wanted to wake up and have everything be all right again. They had lost the person who had provided for them all their lives, and it was all on her shoulders to care for all of them.

She believed Theodore was going to be found, but as time passed, her hopes of finding him began to fade. She didn't want to accept her loss, but it became obvious that Theodore was never coming back.

Thirty-seven years have passed, and Theodore's body was never found. Only the memories of his short life were left for his family to cling to. The memories which were the only thing the aggressors couldn't erase, because they were the only thing his family had left to overshadow their loss.

CHAPTER 13

A Window of Opportunity

Only a fool would say no to someone offering water and food after being left to die in the middle of a desert—only a fool would reject help from someone when he is up to his head in a sinkhole and see no way out!

Opportunities are hard to come by, and when they do, we must take hold of them. I tried everything in my early age, and every time I thought I had it all, something unexpected happened. It was like I was, walking on a long dusty road, and I couldn't see my final destination. Then when I found a place to rest under a tree of some kind, the tree would die. I was forced to move on to the unknown, putting my hope in the One who had promised me that He was going to be with me forever. Although I was left with nothing many times, I never questioned where God was. I had a sense of completeness and assurance that all was well—even when I was sleeping in a back of an abandoned car in a shop where I was working.

After I left home in a hurry and closed my business, I went to the capital city. I was running away from something that I didn't know how to hide from. I first found a church since there the undeniable love from the Father hadn't faded away. No matter where I was, there was the fire of God within me. It wouldn't leave me alone.

There was not much hope in the place I found, but I kept going forward. I did not know God's plan for me. I found work as an apprentice in a body shop, but that wasn't going to be enough to get me a place to live. I ended up sleeping in the cars in the shop.

My mother was worrying even more since she knew it wasn't safe there. She was trying to protect me at all costs, but she had nowhere to hide me anymore. Her fear was that I would be caught by the army or the rebel forces and be forced to fight for one or the other. I don't know how much she was praying for me, but I am sure she was constantly praying for me—and I know her prayers were heard.

There were times when I had to get through two or three checkpoints, and every time I did, I was like a ghost to them. It was like I wasn't there. I never had a problem. Sometimes the officer would skip me and move to the next person in line like he hadn't seen me. I was not trying to hide because I had done something wrong, but I was a youth who could pose a threat to them since I wasn't enlisted in the army. At that age, I had to join the army or the rebels.

Military service wasn't optional, and neither was the other side. There was constant recruiting from both parties, and once one was caught, there was no way out until one was killed or badly injured. For the first time in the nation's history, the army was recruiting women to serve. No youth was safe from either side, and the threat was from all sides.

The other group was terrorizing the nation by killing people in the middle of the night. No civilian felt safe—whether or not they were involved in either of the factions. My mother was always expecting to hear that I had been taken, and was working behind my back to find a way to get me out of the country.

Two months after I had left the house, I decided to see my mother. She was really glad to see me still in one piece. It was just a few months before my eighteenth birthday, and I found out what she had been planning. She had been in touch with one of the people who knew all about the programs that were available for Salvadorians who wanted to migrate to other countries that were taking in refugees. One of them was Mexico. She said, "Tomorrow we are going to see a man who is going to help you get out of this country. I prefer to have you far away than to have you dead."

I kind of liked her idea, but I wasn't eligible to leave

the country on my own because I was a minor. We needed someone who knew all the details.

The next day, we went to get all the information we needed and apply to migrate to another country. To get my passport, I needed to get my mom to sign me off and get my father's death certificate. We hadn't registered my father's death with the coroner's office, and more than two years had passed already. We checked with the man to see what we could do, and we found some people who helped us get things in order. Within two weeks, I had the papers ready for my passport.

Without wasting any time, my mom and I traveled to the capital city to apply for my first passport. She had to sign a release form to validate my application. The man who was guiding me walked me through the whole process. It wasn't easy to make my decision when I knew I was going to leave my mother, siblings, relatives, friends, and everything else. If I stayed, I was going to be responsible for my mother's death and my own. She knew I was going in and out of dangerous places and putting my life at risk.

I knew I had made it to that point because God had a purpose for my life, but that didn't mean I wasn't afraid every time the sun went down. I could probably run fast or hide from danger, but when a death squad was hunting people in the middle of the night, there was no chance to run. I knew God was orchestrating a move for me. The more I wrestled with the idea of getting out of the country

I called home, the more I was hammered by the thought that it was all God's doing. It was God's plan to bring me to another country in fulfilment of His promise. It was not because He couldn't accomplish what He had promised me where I was—He wanted to bless others through me.

After two weeks, we went back to pick my passport. Once I had it in my hand, I was ready to go to the Mexican embassy to apply for my visa. Getting my passport gave me a mixture of emotions. It was like a door had been opened to another world—but I wasn't able to bring anything else with me besides my faith.

On September 15, 1982, El Salvador's Independence Day, I left my beloved country with tears in my eyes. I didn't know if I was ever going to see my loved ones again.

EPILOGUE

As you come to the end of this book, perhaps you have been able to identify yourself in one way or another. Many people who were hurt in one way or another are represented in the pages of this book. People were victims of the war, and others were victimized for other reasons, but as hard it can be to forgive our aggressors, it is not impossible when we let the Holy Spirit take over our pain.

It wasn't easy to forgive the three men who came to my house and snatched away the life of my father, leaving me fatherless. Worst of all is that there wasn't anything I could have done to save him. For many years, I wrestled with unforgiveness. Every time I came across a cop or another military agent, I would feel hate toward them. Even when years had passed, I still kept the faces of those three individuals in my mind. It wasn't easy to erase their faces from my mind. Every time I thought about them, revenge came to my mind.

I couldn't forget what they had done to the person who had given all to raise me. In that one moment, his life was extinguished. I wouldn't have been able to forgive them if it wasn't for the Holy Spirit. He helped me understand that if I didn't forgive them, I was not going to be able to see the kingdom of God.

God showed me that bitterness wasn't His plan for my life. I know it can seem better to take matters into our own hands—and I had a chance to do it—but by doing so, I was going to be stopping the wrath of God from coming down upon those who had wronged me. Vengeance is His, and He will pay it accordingly.

Some people—especially those who lived through those days and lost parents, siblings, and other relatives—need more than words to bring healing to their hearts. Like the man in 2017, in Long Island, New York, who was reliving the nightmare again every time he told the story of burying some of his siblings by himself after he escaped from the army. Thirty-seven years later, he still relives the moment every time he tells the story. He felt like everybody let him down at a young age, and as a result, he didn't trust anyone. In all that time, he hadn't seen his mother because he was afraid to set foot back in his country.

There are thousands of people like him who were psychologically damaged after seeing horrendous crimes. The crimes were purposely committed against innocent people who knew nothing about why they were being murdered. Without an explanation, they were lined up and shot in cold blood.

My grandparents tried to save their sons and offered money in exchange for their lives, but money wasn't powerful enough to stop those bloodthirsty men whose mission was only to kill. Like the lady who had lost her husband and cried out to God, lifting her hands up to the skies and asking why He let those people take away everything she had.

It was hard to watch the damage being done to innocent people, and it was even worse to be part of the victims. We know that there will be casualties in war, but it was an actual case of genocide. No one was held accountable, and that makes it difficult to forgive. Those who committed those crimes will never be held responsible, but when we take the road of forgiveness, we show that we are stronger than those who committed those cowardly acts.

It was difficult to understand God's plan for my life in the midst of all the destruction, but I understood that someone was watching over me. When I lost everything, I still had something to hang on to. I knew that the grace of God was infinite—and He was going to make things right for me.

In my darkest moments, when I thought I was at the bottom of the pit, the light of the day began shining on me again. Even when I thought the storm was over and began enjoying the prosperity that came along for only short while, something inside me never let me deny the existence of God. Even when I had a reason to curse the people who took all I had, I chose to forgive them because the Holy Spirit led me to forgiveness. Just as he has done it for me, I am sure He wants to free those who still can't figure out how to forgive monstrous crimes like that. It sounds too easy to act like it never happened, especially when all the crimes were left unpunished, but I'm sure that God is just and nothing on this earth goes unnoticed.

Thirty-five years passed before I was able to go back to my home village. I felt a tremendous urgency to go back. In almost every dream, I found myself in my beloved home village. I knew I had to go back and do something before I lost sight of my father's grave.

After all those years, I managed to put things together with the idea of moving the three bodies to a cemetery that were buried in the same grave in our backyard. I was excited to do something for me, my siblings, and the new generation.

From Canada, I traveled back to the village that my eyes saw the first time they opened. Things had changed, but in my mind, it was all like it was when I was a kid. My biggest surprise was when a family team assessed whether it was going to be possible to move the remains. My beautiful village had been completely destroyed. The paradise that once was, had been turned into a desolate place.

Only a few villagers were living there. They didn't make up for the number of people who used to live there, and the absence of people made the place like a graveyard. I was stunned to see how time had changed things. I tried to figure out where my house used to be, but it was impossible. I couldn't even find the foundation or the retaining wall behind it. It all had been leveled, and I wasn't able to find my way out. In my mind, nothing had changed, but nature had reclaimed what belonged to it—and it had left only the memories of the good times and beauty in the minds of those who used to lived there.

Printed in the United States
By Bookmasters